THE ENCYCLOPEDIA OF THE TED BUNDY MURDERS

"Sullivan's A-to-Z coverage of Ted Bundy provides a solid guide to the people and places that define the man and the monster ... an extensive reference tool on one of the world's most infamous serial killers."

—**Katherine Ramsland**, author of *Confession of a Serial Killer: The Untold Story of Dennis Rader, the BTK Killer.*

KEVIN SULLIVAN

WildBluePress.com

THE ENCYCLOPEDIA OF THE TED BUNDY MURDERS
published by:
WILDBLUE PRESS
P.O. Box 102440
Denver, Colorado 80250

Publisher Disclaimer: Any opinions, statements of fact or fiction, descriptions, dialogue, and citations found in this book were provided by the author, and are solely those of the author. The publisher makes no claim as to their veracity or accuracy, and assumes no liability for the content.

Copyright 2020 by Kevin M. Sullivan

All rights reserved. No part of this book may be reproduced in any form or by any means without the prior written consent of the Publisher, excepting brief quotes used in reviews.

WILDBLUE PRESS is registered at the U.S. Patent and Trademark Offices.

ISBN 978-1-948239-61-5 Trade Paperback

ISBN 978-1-948239-60-8 eBook

Cover design © 2019 WildBlue Press. All rights reserved.

Interior Formatting/Book Cover Design by Elijah Toten
www.totencreative.com

THE ENCYCLOPEDIA OF THE TED BUNDY MURDERS

TABLE OF CONTENTS

Preface	7
A	9
B	16
C	32
D	49
E	60
F	64
G	70
H	77
I	91
J	96
K	97
L	110
M	119
N	133
O	140
P	145
R	159
S	170
T	195
U	203
V	204
W	210
Y	218
Z	220
Afterword	221
Entry Index	225

For my grandchildren...
Isabella, Connor, James, Calliope, Stella

PREFACE

In late April 2019, and only days after my fourth book in my series of books on Ted Bundy was published, a Facebook friend by the name of Michael Reinhart, contacted me with a most curious question: had I thought about writing an encyclopedia on the Ted Bundy murder case, and I told him no. Indeed, the thought of it was so currently out of the realm of reality for me, that there just wasn't any way I'd consider it. But I did thank him for the suggestion, and we both agreed that it was right to set the idea aside for the time being. Truth be told, Michael had considered doing it himself. But he's so busy with current projects – with others in the pipeline waiting for him –, that it was only natural he'd think of me. A great idea, we both agreed, and we let it drop right there.

However, over the next several days, every time our conversation crossed my mind, I had this unmistakable good feeling about the project, and so after about three days, I decided to contact my publisher and run the idea by them. And immediately, they loved the idea. Well, that response, coupled with my "good feelings" has allowed me to take the step that's led me to write the Encyclopedia of the Ted Bundy Murders. It is, without question, the go-to guide into all things Ted Bundy, the innocent victims who fell by his hands, and the hundreds of people and dozens of locations that became intertwined, and sometimes synonymous with, the life and times of Ted Bundy. For those desiring to know the thousands of interconnected facts of the case, and what has transpired with all those involved over the years, this is the book for you.

AFRICANO, JULIUS VICTOR

Victor Africano (1938-2002) was the lead defense attorney for Ted Bundy in the Kimberly Diane Leach trial. Although Africano would mount a splendid defense to save his client, the scales of justice would go against Ted Bundy, and it would be for this murder that Bundy would be executed on January 24, 1989. Africano is buried in Live Oak Cemetery in Suwannee County, Florida, not too far from where the body of 12-year-old Kimberly Leach, Bundy's last victim, was discovered.

AIME, JAMES "JIM" JUNIOR

Jim Aime (1928-1987), father of Bundy victim, Laura Ann Aime, and the one who identified her body. Speaking to a friend, while he was driving past the location where Laura's body was found, Jim Aime said, "My little baby was up there all by herself and there was nothing I could do to help her." Incidentally, that friend was Jim Massie, a probation and parole officer from Louisville, Kentucky, who was also a friend of Detective Jerry Thompson, and was the link to how I met retired Detective Thompson. You'll also find that above quote in Ron Holmes' book, *Serial Murder*, as Massie and Holmes worked together on some projects pertaining to Ted Bundy and serial murder.

AIME, LAURA ANN

On Halloween night of 1974, Laura Ann Aime (1957-1974) left on foot a party in the city of Orem, Utah, and after stopping to purchase cigarettes, started hitchhiking on what police believed was one of "the darker portions of Highway 89." It would be in this area that Ted Bundy would stop his VW and give young Laura a ride. Here the information goes dark, and her body wasn't discovered until Thanksgiving Day, November 27, 1974. Bundy, who had a habit of occasionally leaving bodies close to roads where they might be easily found, did so with Aime. Around 9:00 a.m. on that cool sunny Thanksgiving morning, two Brigham Young University students parked their car in the lot of the Timpanogos Visitor Welcome Center and headed out on a hiking trail. After going about 500 yards, they spotted the naked body of a female lying just off the roadway. The startled couple ran back to their car and drove straight to the Ranger station to report what they'd seen. The body was that of Laura Aime.

AIME, SHIRLY TOLTON

Shirly Aime (1934-2011) was the mother of Laura Ann Aime.

ALAMEDA JUNIOR HIGH SCHOOL

Alameda Junior High School, located at 845 McKinley Avenue in Pocatello, Idaho, was, on May 6, 1975, the scene of an abduction carried out by Ted Bundy. Bundy had come to the city the day before to hunt college coeds at the nearby university, but was unsuccessful. The next morning, Bundy left the Holiday Inn, located some two miles away, and began trolling for a victim. Within a short time, he pulled up to the school just as 12-year-old Lynette Culver came out the front doors of the school, and Bundy waved her over to his car. Because it was lunch time, many students were also standing around the front of the school, or heading to a nearby park, but no one noticed Culver enter Bundy's VW. The two returned to his room at the Holiday Inn where Bundy would drown the young girl in the bathtub before having sexual intercourse with her dead body.

ANDERSON, C.L.

C.L. Anderson, better known as Andy Anderson, was a firefighter living in Lake City, Florida. On the morning of February 9, 1974, as he was heading home from his overnight shift, he noticed a white van that was stopped (angled) and blocking traffic in the road that runs directly in front of Lake City Junior High. Assessing the situation, he noticed a man (Bundy) who appeared to be angrily leading a young girl to the passenger side of the van. His first thought was, "daddy's going to take the little girl home and give her a spanking." That little girl was Kimberly Diane Leach, 12, and would be Ted Bundy's final victim.

ANDERSON, CHIEF DEAN O.

Chief Dean O. Anderson, of the Bountiful Police Department, headed up the investigation into the disappearance and presumed abduction of Debra Kent from Bountiful, Utah on November 8, 1974, after she left the play at Viewmont High School to pick up her brother from a nearby roller rink. Bundy nabbed her as she was attempting to reach her parents' car, and she may have done so. But Bundy was able to attack her before she got inside the car. A number of homes and apartments across the street and to the side of the school, would hear a scream around this same time, which of course, was Debra Kent.

ANDERSON, LARRY

Larry Anderson came into contact with Ted Bundy after Bundy sought out fellowship with the Mormon Church in Salt Lake City, Utah. Larry and three other men lived in a house at 629 Eleventh Avenue in the city, and Larry, along with housemate, John Homer, were stake missionaries with the Mormon Church, and it was their job to mentor Bundy and teach him the ways of the church. Larry told me when we first talked, that he had been approached by a national magazine just after Bundy's execution on January 24, 1989 to tell his story, but he turned them down.

Larry's story is quite interesting, and while I can't reproduce the entire story here, I would be remiss if I didn't share some of it for this in-depth encyclopedia. What follows is from *The Trail of Ted Bundy: Digging Up the Untold Stories* and pertains to what was happening just after Bundy's arrest in October 1975 for the kidnapping of Carol DaRonch. Like everyone else who knew Bundy, they didn't believe the allegations against him were true, and this was the exact and normal reaction from Bundy's friends back in Washington State when they heard the disturbing news. Even so, the wheels of reason began to turn in everyone's mind, and at that point, it would begin to explain certain things that Bundy had previously said to them, or demonstrated in his actions. Here are two such cases from the book:

But there were things that arose that Anderson would look back on after Bundy's arrest, and they were very telling. For example, after the attempted abduction of Carol DaRonch, a composite drawing of the attacker had been published in the local papers. One night while Bundy was at the house, located at 629 Eleventh Ave., Salt Lake City, Utah, the composite drawing was being passed around, and Bundy joined in the conversation. According to Anderson, as they were discussing how a person could pull off something like this, Bundy laughed and said, "I can tell you exactly how a person could do it," and then launched into how he'd worked with the governor of Washington, the time he spent on the Seattle Crime Commission, and how he learned about the various police jurisdictions, and how they don't always cooperate with each other. And then he uttered something that would become chillingly clear later on: "You could kidnap (a victim) from one location, kill in another, put the clothes (of the victim) in a different jurisdiction, the body in another, and none of it would be connected."

And again, when the need to kill had overwhelmed Bundy, causing him to cancel a trip that he had initiated:

Other incidents would stand out as well. Larry Anderson remembers when he and Ted planned a trip to Vail, Colorado, for some skiing in the winter months in early 1975. When the day arrived, Anderson was waiting for Bundy outside, packed with all his equipment and ready to go. But when Bundy showed up, he backed out of his commitment, saying, "Can I go by myself?" before quickly adding, "I need some time alone." Anderson remarked "I was waiting for him on the curb ... He just drove up and canceled." Anderson noted that he would later learn the time of Bundy's "alone" trip coincided with one of the Colorado murders.

ASPEN, COLORADO

Aspen, Colorado played a pivotal role in the Ted Bundy Murders. On January 12, 1975, Bundy abducted young Caryn Campbell from the Wildwood Inn in Snowmass Village. Using crutches and carrying ski boots, Bundy had his eye on another woman when Caryn Campbell offered Bundy assistance. After helping Bundy to his car that was parked in the large side parking lot, Bundy struck her with the ski boots and threw her into his VW. Her frozen and partially eaten body would be located weeks later just a few feet off Owl Creek Road and some 2.8 miles from the Wildwood Inn. Aspen would also take center stage during Bundy's first escape in the state when he jumped out of the second story window from the Aspen Courthouse. Bundy was recaptured less than a week later.

Aspen Courthouse in Aspen, Colorado. In June 1977, Bundy would jump out the far-left window on the top floor to make his escape into the wilds of Colorado.

AUGERSON, OFFICER TERRANCE

Officer Terrance Augerson of the Seattle Police Department, was one of the officers who was assigned to follow Ted Bundy during Bundy's two months back in the Seattle. Bundy arrived in Seattle in November 1975, but police did not locate him until December 1st. Bundy would leave Seattle for Salt Lake City, Utah in early February 1976 to stand trial for the kidnapping of Carol DaRonch. Officer Augerson is one of a number of officers who appear in the often fast-paced reports pertaining to the surveillance of Bundy during this period. This is a small portion of one of his reports, dated December 5, 1975:

Our subject gave the w/ f a kiss then the w/ f gave our subject a big hug. The subject then walked around the north side of the residence with w/ f 9 while the w/ f 20's departed S/ W bound. The subject & the w/ f 9 then drove to the front of University Hospital and picked up w/ f 20's wearing beige clothing. Subject then drove S/B on I-5 from Montlake to same exit. Subject pulled to curb and we lost him for approximately 3 minutes due to very heavy traffic. I located his veh. Parked & unoccupied at Occidental & Wash. Parked at a meter. At approx. 1810 subject returned to his veh. with same two females & drove around downtown. He pulled to curb several times and circled block. Subject then drove N/B on I-5 to Worth gate and entered shopping mall. Subject accompanied by same two w/f entered his veh.... then drove N/B on I-5 to 145th exit. Subject drove to Big Boy Restaurant at 145 & Aurora & parked in rear.

AUSTIN, DR. VAN O.

Dr. Van O. Austin was a Utah psychiatrist assigned to evaluate Ted Bundy for a pre-sentence investigation report after Bundy's conviction for the kidnapping of Carol DaRonch. Austin would work closely with Dr. Al Carlisle, the psychologist who worked with Bundy; and

who Bundy liked and learned to trust. Both Austin and Carlisle understood that Bundy was trying very hard to keep his true nature hidden from them and said so in their reports.

AYNESWORTH, HUGH GRANT

Hugh Aynesworth is an American journalist, and co-author along with Stephen Michaud, of *The Only Living Witness: The True Story of Serial Sex Killer Ted Bundy* and *Ted Bundy: Conversations with a Killer*. Aynesworth, whose career spans over five decades, was on hand for many of the important events in Dallas, Texas during the assassination of President John F. Kennedy, on November 22, 1963.

BAILESS, PROFESSOR TIM

Professor Tim Bailess was one of Ted Bundy's professors at the University of Utah School of Law.

BAIRD, NANCY

Nancy Baird, 23, is a suspected Ted Bundy victim. On July 4, 1975, Nancy was working at a Fina gas station some 25 miles north of Salt Lake City, in Davis County. Business that day had apparently been brisk, but around 5:30 p.m., Nancy Baird suddenly disappeared. Her employer would tell authorities that her car was still there, locked, and in the same space where she'd parked it that morning. Her purse, along with the money from her recently cashed check, was found undisturbed behind the counter. The body of Nancy Baird has never been located. And while this murder cannot be officially linked to Ted Bundy, in this writer's opinion, he's likely her killer.

BALDRIDGE, DETECTIVE WILLIAM

Detective William Baldridge, with the Pitkin County Sheriff's Office, was the first individual to contact Detective Michael Fisher of the District Attorney's Office, which brought Fisher front and center into the investigation of the disappearance of Caryn Campbell from the Wildwood Inn in Snowmass, Colorado. On March 11, 1976, both Fisher and Baldridge would interview Ted Bundy concerning Campbell's abduction and murder.

BALL, BRENDA CAROL

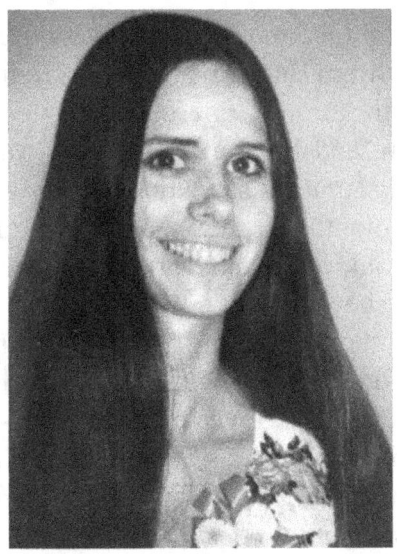

Brenda Ball

Brenda Carol Ball, 22 and a Ted Bundy victim, disappeared from the Flame Tavern in the early morning hours of June 1, 1974. The Flame Tavern was located in Burien, which is south of Seattle, and it's a place that Brenda Ball felt comfortable and was a regular. There are two stories circulating concerning how she was captured by Ted Bundy. The most credible is that she asked a male friend at the tavern if he could give her a ride home, but he told Brenda he wasn't going in that direction. After this, she departed the Flame and started hitchhiking, and it was Bundy who gave her a ride. The other scenario has her leaving with a man and ostensibly getting her ride home. On March 1, 1975, the cranium, minus the lower mandible, of Brenda Ball was discovered on Taylor Mountain in Washington State. The rest of her remains have never been recovered.

BARDOLE, FRANCINE

Francine Bardole and her son, Larry, had numerous interactions with Ted Bundy while he was living in Utah. The connection came through one of Bundy local girlfriend's, Leslie Knutson, and her son, Josh, who was friends with Francine's son. Knutson's relationship with Bundy lasted a number of months during the spring and summer of 1975, but it would ultimately fail as Knutson saw aspects of Bundy that she didn't like which caused her to end the relationship. Francine also saw troubling signs, and in fact, some of the oddities they witnessed would make perfect sense after Bundy was revealed as a multi-state killer of women. Francine Bardole's story can be found in my book, *Ted Bundy's Murderous Mysteries: The Many Victims of America's Most Infamous Serial Killer.*

BARNARD, KENT

April 17, 1974, was Kent Barnard's birthday, and he had made plans to drive over the Cascade Mountains to Central Washington State College in Ellensburg, Washington, to visit his girlfriend. Kent had no idea what he'd be seeing that day, and how this particular day would forever stand out in his mind. Barnard said he first spotted the man with "his left arm in a dark blue sling" around 2:00 p.m. as he and his girlfriend passed by the library. The man was standing toward the front of the building and next to a bicycle rack. Barnard would spot him once more around 9:30 p.m. in front of Barge Hall, where Deanna, his girlfriend was having a class. Bundy had spent all day hunting the campus but without success. That would change around 10:00 p.m. when he tricked Susan Rancourt to follow him to his car that was parked in an isolated area of the campus. Kent Barnard would see Bundy again that night, but he wouldn't realize it for several years. As he drove back home that night, he spotted a "set of small round taillights about 200 yards up a logging road on the north side of I-90." Unbeknownst to Barnard, he had just seen the car that held the dying or dead body of Susan Rancourt. The full story of Kent Barnard can be found in my book, *The Trail of Ted Bundy: Digging Up the Untold Stories*.

BARTHOLOMEW, CAROL

In March 1975, Carol Hall (soon to be Bartholomew), was attending a birthday party in Salt Lake City, Utah where Ted Bundy was also present. As she stood in the kitchen doing dishes, Bundy walked up to her and offered to help. Because Carol's camera was lying nearby, she asked Wynn Bartholomew to take their picture. Bundy, playfully pointing the rinsing gun at her, smiled for the camera. This photograph has been seen by millions, and Carol's full story can be found in *The Trail of Ted Bundy: Digging Up the Untold Stories*.

BARTHOLOMEW, WYNN

Wynn Bartholomew (1947-2013), like Bundy, was a law school student, but was two years ahead of him. Nevertheless, they knew each other, and Bartholomew remembered seeing Bundy "in the winter of 1975, looking haggard, with bags under his eyes and crimson red scratches branded across his cheeks and neck." Bartholomew joked with Bundy, asking him if he'd had a rough date, and Bundy quickly blamed it on a tree branch. Bartholomew did not believe Bundy's explanation. He would go on to marry Carol Hall, who shares a famous photo with Ted Bundy, where it appears Bundy is helping her do the dishes. The photo came about when Carol asked Wynn to grab her camera and take a picture of them. Wynn did as he was asked, and in the near future, Wynn and Carol began to date, and they would go on to have six sons, and nine grandchildren.

BATTEMA, NANCY

Nancy Battema would spend the afternoon of July 14, 1974 at Lake Sammamish State Park, with her boyfriend, Bob Sargent, Kenneth Little, and Little's girlfriend, Denise Naslund. At approximately 4:20 that afternoon, as Denise was coming out of the women's restroom, she encountered Ted Bundy who was looking to abduct his second victim from that lake that day. Using an unknown ruse, Denise followed Bundy to his VW parked nearby, and most likely left the park with a promise from Bundy that they'd return shortly. The partial remains of Denise Naslund would later be discovered at what is known as Ted Bundy's Issaquah Dump Site.

BEAL, DETECTIVE IRA

Detective Ira Beal was the lead investigator with the Bountiful Police Department for the disappearance of Debra Kent, who was abducted by Ted Bundy on the evening of November 8, 1974. Debra brought her parents to Viewmont High School to see the school's production of *The Redhead*. She left before the play was out so she could pick up her brother from a nearby roller rink. Bundy abducted her before she reached her car. Beal would work closely with Detective Jerry Thompson of the Salt Lake County Sheriff's Office, after Bundy became their prime suspect in the kidnapping of Carol DaRonch. DaRonch was attacked earlier the same night but escaped from Bundy after Bundy slapped both handcuffs on the same wrist. And this escape meant Debra Kent would die.

BEER, JOHN

John Beer was a teacher at Wilson High School in Tacoma, Washington when Bundy was a student there, and he remembered him well. In a July 3, 1986 interview with the *Tacoma News Tribune*, Beer, who was one of Bundy's teachers, said he remembered Bundy and spoke of his time there when he said, "he was a better-than-average student, but not a standout." He would also comment to the reporter the feelings he and others shared at Wilson High concerning their former student: "There hasn't been a swell of Ted Bundy sympathy that I know of.... This thing has gone on far too long. If he's not executed, we should look again to the American Jurisprudence system."

BLACK, CARLA JEAN

After the attack on Florida State University's Chi Omega Sorority in the early morning hours of February 15, 1978, Carla Jean Black came forward to tell the police of the odd man (Bundy) whom she saw at the disco, Sherrod's, around 12:30 a.m. and only hours before the murders. According to Black's Tallahassee Police Report, his "dress and age along with his appearance, i.e. greasy looking appearance, made him stand out to her. Moreover, this subject kept staring at her and she was afraid he was going to ask her to dance.... Ms. Black states that he kept staring at her, along with many other persons, and that his mannerisms seemed to be more a 'rude type of looking' 'that he appeared to be smirking' or 'that he felt superior' or a 'I know something that you don't know attitude.'"

BLACKBURN, DONALD EDWIN

Donald Edwin Blackburn (1922-2010) was the father of Janice Ann Ott.

BLACKBURN, FEROL LORRAINE

Ferol Lorraine Blackburn (1921-2018) was the mother of Janice Ann Ott.

BLAKEY, MILTON K.

Milton K. Blakey was the Deputy District Attorney located in Colorado Springs, Colorado. However, because he was going to be prosecuting Ted Bundy, he was transferred to Aspen, Colorado to work closely with Detective Michael Fisher who had been busy building a case against the killer. Blakey was also responsible for having Detective Fisher investigate the homicides in Utah that Bundy was suspected of committing, and if they found similarities between the murders in Utah with those of Colorado, the prosecution believed they could build a better case against Bundy for a jury trial. The court, however, would ultimately disallow the prosecution's request to enter similar transactions into the proceedings.

BODIFORD, DETECTIVE STEVE

Detective Steve Bodiford was an investigator with the Leon County Sheriff's Office, and one of three Det's that interviewed Bundy in Pensacola after his arrest in that city on February 15, 1978. When arrested, Bundy gave his name as Kenneth Misner, but that was proved false when the real Kenneth Misner, a University of Florida track star, contacted authorities. Because Bundy had stolen 21 credit cards from Tallahassee, some of which belonged to FSU coeds, the Tallahassee police were contacted. This brought Detective Don Patchen of the Tallahassee Police Department and Detective Steve Bodiford of the Leon County Sheriff's Office, to Pensacola, Florida where they, along with Detective Norman Chapman of the Pensacola PD, began grilling the suspect then referred to as "Mr. Doe." Bundy would shortly identify himself, and would ultimately be transferred to a steel reinforced maximum-security cell in the Leon County Jail. Bodiford and Patchen would continue interrogation of Ted Bundy after he was transferred to Tallahassee.

BOISE, IDAHO

Boise, Idaho plays a part in the Ted Bundy murders due to a hitchhiker he picked up on the outskirts of the city on Monday, September 2, 1974. It was Labor Day, and Bundy left Seattle that morning after having breakfast with Liz, her daughter, and Marylynn Chino on Chino's houseboat. His destination was Salt Lake City, Utah where he'd enrolled in the University of Utah School of Law. But Bundy was all about killing, and as Bundy entered the suburbs of Boise, he spotted a young woman hitchhiking at the top of an on-ramp. She was carrying a green backpack; Bundy would later confess they travelled for three or four hours on I-84 before taking a small road that led to a river where he killed her. He then told authorities he slid her nude body into the river and her body was never found.

BOOKS

What follows are the books considered the mainstream books on Ted Bundy:

Dekle, George R. Sr. *The Last Murder: The Investigation, Prosecution, and Execution of Ted Bundy* (2011)

Kendall, Elizabeth. *The Phantom Prince: My Life with Ted Bundy* (1981)

Keppel, Robert D., and William J. Burns. *The Riverman: Ted Bundy and I Hunt for the Green River Killer* (1995)

Keppel, Robert D. and Michaud, Stephen G. *Terrible Secrets: Ted Bundy on Serial Murder* (2011)

Larsen, Richard W. *Bundy: The Deliberate Stranger* (1980)

Lewis, Dorothy Otnow M.D. *Guilty by Reason of Insanity: A Psychiatrist Explores the Minds of Killers* (1998)

Michaud, Stephen G., and Hugh Aynesworth. *The Only Living Witness: The True Story of Serial Sex Killer Ted Bundy* (1983)

---------. *Ted Bundy: Conversations with a Killer* (2000)

Morris, Rebecca. *Ted and Ann: The Mystery of a Missing Child and Her Neighbor Ted Bundy* (2013)

Nelson, Polly. *Defending the Devil: My Story as Ted Bundy's Last lawyer* (1994)

Rule, Ann. *The Stranger Beside Me* (1980)

Sullivan, Kevin M. *The Bundy Murders: A Comprehensive History* (2009)

Von Drehle, David. *Among the Lowest of the Dead: The Culture of Death Row* (1995)

Winn, Steve and David Merrill. *Ted Bundy: The Killer Next Door* (1980)

BOONE, CAROL

Carol Boone met Ted Bundy while in Washington State, but because of his ongoing relationship with Liz Kloepfer, she understood their relationship wasn't going to go anywhere. However, after Liz had pretty much ended it with Bundy, he began communicating with Carol and she visited him at the Garfield County Jail shortly before Bundy escaped and made his way to Florida. Smitten by Bundy and believing in his innocence, she would eventually move to Florida to be near him. And in a bizarre occurrence, on February 9, 1980, two years to the day from the murder of Kimberly Leach, Bundy proposed marriage to Carol while he cross examined her during the penalty phase of the Kimberly Leach trial, and she accepted. This was completely legal in Florida, and because a Notary Public was present, they became husband and wife. Later, Bundy figured out a way for them to consummate their vows, and it is unknown how many times this occurred. However, on one occasion it resulted in pregnancy and the eventual birth of their daughter, Rosa.

BOUNTIFUL, UTAH

Bountiful, Utah, located 11.4 miles north of Salt Lake City, played host to the brazen abduction of Debra Kent, 17, from the parking lot of Viewmont High School around 10:30 p.m. on November 8, 1974, as she left a school play to pick up her brother from a nearby roller rink.

BOWMAN, MARGARET

Margaret Bowman

Margaret Bowman (1957-1978), 21, was one of four women attacked by Ted Bundy while they slept in the Chi Omega Sorority house in Tallahassee, Florida in the early morning hours of January 15, 1978. Bundy severely injured Margaret with a log and then strangled her to death. According to the investigator who first viewed the body, "... Ms. Bowman had received a crushing blow to her right forehead coupled with what appeared to be to puncture wounds in the same vicinity. Massive bleeding occurred from both the forehead and the right ear. Additionally, Ms.

Bowman's neck appeared to be disjointed leading this writer to believe there was a possible neck fracture. Ms. Bowman's body was relatively warm to the touch and her eyes were glassy with pupils dilated."

BRANNON, OFFICER OSCAR

Officer Oscar Brannon, of the Tallahassee Police Department, was the first patrolman to respond to the Chi Omega sorority house after the attack of January 15, 1978. Arriving with him were officers from the Florida State University Police, as well as ambulances from nearby Tallahassee Memorial Hospital. As Brannon entered the premises it was, by his report, 3:22 a.m. Brannon was also the first officer to speak with Nita Neary about the man she saw coming down the steps (Bundy), and exit the front door. As the second officer to view the body of Margaret Bowman, he said the following: Margaret Elizabeth Bowman was found face down on her bed [with] no vital signs present and no hope of gaining any.

BRIGHAM YOUNG UNIVERSITY

Brigham Young University (BYU), located some 45 miles south of Salt Lake City in Provo, Utah, was the site of the abduction of fifteen-year-old, Susan Curtis, who was attending a youth conference in the summer of 1975. In an odd twist, young Susan Curtis was in the audience watching the play, *The Red Head*, at Viewmont High School in Bountiful, Utah, on the night Ted Bundy was hunting for a victim there. Bundy would capture Debra Kent in the parking lot of the high school after she left the play to pick up her brother at a nearby roller rink. As Bundy sped away with his latest victim, he and Susan Curtis were destined to meet again. For more on the murder of Susan Curtis, see Curtis, Susan, this book.

BURNHAM, STEVE

At approximately 12:30 a.m., on June 11, 1974, Steve Burnham, a member of the Phi Kappa Sigma fraternity, was walking home on 17th Avenue, when he spotted a man sporting a leg cast and hobbling on crutches while attempting to hold onto a briefcase. The man was Ted Bundy, and he was attempting to cross 17th where it intersects with 47th Street. Burnham, who believed the man was legitimately struggling, left the sidewalk on the opposite side of the street and jaywalked to reach the other side and offer help. But before Burnham could reach him, a woman, coming from the opposite end of the crosswalk, reached Bundy and she carried his briefcase across the street and gave it back once they reached the other side. Seeing this, Burnham continued toward home.

BROWNE, JOHN HENRY

While John Henry Browne was Ted Bundy's attorney in Washington State, their association would continue throughout the remainder of Bundy's life, including his years on Florida's death row. Indeed, Browne would work very hard, along with others, trying to get Bundy to accept life in prison in the state, and all he had to do was confess to the Florida murders and say nothing else. It proved too much for Bundy, who rejected the offer, with fatal consequences.

BUNDY, GLENN

Glenn Bundy (born 1954) was the half-brother of Ted Bundy, and apparently Bundy got along well with him. After Bundy left Seattle for Salt Lake City, Utah on September 2, 1974 to attend law school, he packed his small VW Beetle with as many items as he could carry and headed towards his future. Part of that future was the killing of an Idaho hitchhiker later that day when he picked her up on the outskirts of Boise, Idaho. However, Bundy had much more to move, so he returned to Seattle on the 18th of the month and with the help of brother Glenn and Bundy's friend, Marlin Vortman, they packed an older model truck Bundy had purchased for the return trip. Glenn would accompany Bundy back to Utah to help him unload everything and carry it up to his second-floor apartment at 565 First Avenue. Glenn then caught a flight back to Seattle.

BUNDY, LINDA

Linda Bundy (born 1952) was the half-sister of Ted Bundy. After Bundy was convicted in the DaRonch kidnapping, and the pre-sentence investigation was being prepared for the judge, Linda Bundy took that opportunity to write the judge explaining what a good person her brother was, and how he couldn't be involved with such things. And of course, no one could blame her or any other person writing such letters to the judge, because from their perspective, it couldn't be true about the one they loved.

BUNDY, LOUISE

Louise Bundy (1924–2012) was the mother of Ted Bundy. A strong woman, Louise would believe in her son's innocence up until Ted told the world otherwise. A note: in my years studying the case, Bundy, his family, and all those involved, I would occasionally hear unkind comments directed toward Louise, which I found perplexing, as there's nothing either in the record or the testimony of those who knew the Bundy family, that Louise was anything but a loving mother. And sometimes, the same criticisms are directed at the family. And again, I have found the "charges" against Louise Bundy and her family both unfair and unfounded. Whatever transformed Ted Bundy into an insatiable killer of women and young girls, it had absolutely nothing to do with how he was raised by Johnny or Louise, nor did the interactions he had with Glenn, Richard, Sandra or Linda point him to a life of violence and murder. Those who believe otherwise are mistaken.

BUNDY, RICHARD

Richard Bundy (born 1961) was the youngest of the Bundy children, and Ted would later offer to a Probation and Parole officer in Utah that he felt a special closeness to Richard, as a big brother might feel protective of a younger sibling.

BUNDY, SANDRA

Sandra Bundy (born 1956) was a half-sister of Ted Bundy.

BUNDY, JOHNNY CULPEPPER

Johnny Culpepper Bundy (1921–2007), was the husband of Louise and the adoptive father of Ted Bundy. From all reports, Johnny Bundy was a good father to all of his children, including little Teddy. However, it's clear Ted became somewhat combative with Johnny during his teenage years because he believed himself to be intellectually superior. This caused Johnny frustration, and on at least one occasion it got the better of him. According to a friend of Bundy's, after one of Ted's verbal assaults, Johnny took a swing at him but missed. In contrast, it appears in his later years (even during his years of murder) he showed more respect to Johnny, and there's nothing in the record or the testimonies of those who knew them that points to Bundy antagonizing Johnny as an adult. Indeed, both Johnny and Louise would remain committed to their son to the end, and Johnny would convey to a reporter how hard it was dealing with what had happened with Ted.

BURR, ANN MARIE

Ann Marie Burr (1953–1961) was only eight-years-old when someone led her away from her Tacoma, Washington home at 3009 North 14th Street, in the early morning hours of September 1, 1961. A storm had come through the city earlier that night, and because of the late August heat, Ann Marie's two older siblings slept in the basement, while the parents, Donald and Beverly Burr, remained in their first-floor bedroom. Ann Marie would pass the night upstairs with her little sister, Mary. At some point in the middle of the night, Mary, whose arm was in a cast, woke up crying, and Ann Marie took her downstairs to see her mother. Entering the bedroom, they awakened Beverly Burr who calmed the child, and then had Ann Marie take her back to bed.

The Ann Marie Burr home at 3009 North 14th Street, Tacoma, Washington

Within two to three hours of this, an intruder would enter the Burr home through an unlocked window on the side of the house. When Beverly Burr awakened around 5:00 a.m., she found the front door standing open and Ann Marie was nowhere to be found. Was Ann Marie Burr a victim of Ted Bundy? There is a very incriminating statement made by Bundy in the mid-1980s that strongly points in this direction. However, there are also more than a few denials by the killer that he had nothing to do with her disappearance. In the end, we'll probably never know one way or the other. The remains of Ann Marie Burr have never been recovered.

BURR, BEVERLY

Beverly Burr (1928–2008) was the mother of Ann Marie Burr who was kidnapped from their Tacoma, Washington home in the early hours of September 1, 1961. It is likely she was murdered soon after she was taken, and Ted Bundy may have played a part in her death. It is of interest to note too that when I was doing research for my book, *The Bundy Murders: A Comprehensive History*, I had the opportunity to interview Beverly Burr by phone one day, and she was both pleasant and kind to me even though I was asking her about the disappearance of Ann Marie. During our conversation, she told me a story that I would like to record for posterity here, which I believe will be interesting, and one we can all identify with. Beverly said that at some point after the murders, she would occasionally see Louise and Johnny Bundy out together, and that these "sightings" or encounters were extremely brief. However, she also confided that when she and her husband Donald took a tour bus on a trip out of Tacoma (she never said what the destination happened to be), she spotted Johnny and Louise Bundy sitting towards the front of the bus, and it made her very uncomfortable. I told her I understood completely.

BURR, DONALD

Donald Burr (1925–2003) was the father of kidnap and murder victim, Ann Marie Burr.

CAMPBELL, CARYN EILEEN

Caryn Campbell (1951–1975), 23, was a nurse from Michigan who was an unlikely victim of Ted Bundy. She had come to Snowmass, Colorado in January, 1975 with her boyfriend, Dr. Raymond Gadowski, his two children, and another physician friend of theirs by the name of Rosenthall. Ted Bundy, who had literally run himself out of Utah because of the manhunt for the killer of women in the state, had branched out to Colorado to seek more victims. The following information concerning Caryn's abduction came from a news conference given by Colorado Investigator Michael Fisher on January 25, 1989 and published in *The Aspen Times*. On January 12, 1975, Bundy would spend several hours driving around Aspen before heading up "amongst the lodges." as an *Aspen Times* article stated, and it would be here that Bundy would begin hobbling on crutches while carrying (and probably rather badly) ski boots. It was his aim to draw the attention of compassionate women who might render assistance to a man obviously having a difficult time.

The sunken fireplace at the Wildwood Inn where Dr. Gadowski and his two children waited while Caryn Campbell retrieved a magazine from their room.

The outdoor pool at the Wildwood Inn in Snowmass, Colorado.

And so, in the early evening, Bundy found himself waiting near the outdoor heated pool at the Wildwood Inn, trying to attract the attention of a woman who paid him no attention at all. And then, Caryn Campbell, while walking across the second-floor outdoor hallway, spotted Bundy through the wafting clouds of steam coming from the outdoor heated pool, and seeing he was in need, asked him if he needed help. Bundy acknowledged he did, and within moments, Caryn and Bundy were on their way to the large parking lot on the side of the Wildwood Inn. Once they reached his VW, Bundy hit Caryn with the ski boots and then threw her into the car. Once inside, he would have had to hit her at least once more with the crowbar before he could subdue her. Towards the end of the news conference, Fisher was asked if Bundy had sexually assaulted Caryn Campbell, but here he hedged a bit, no doubt to protect her family. However, nineteen years later, as I was working with Mike while writing my book, *The Bundy Murders: A Comprehensive History*, he admitted that Bundy, after striking Caryn in the head with the crowbar, admitted, "I did my thing right there in the car." His "thing" was the sexual assault of Caryn Campbell.

CANNON, LOUISE

Louise Cannon was a teller in a bank located close to the University of Utah law school, and only about one block away from the apartment Bundy rented after he moved out of the rooming house at 565 First Avenue. Bundy chose this new location because he'd been forced to sell his beloved VW Bug to pay his attorney bills, and this apartment at 364 Douglas Avenue, would put him in walking distance of the school. Bundy also chose a new bank branch because of its convenient location. It's clear his desire was to get to know her through dating, and had no intention of murdering her. But things would not go Bundy's way in the matter, and their ongoing interaction would abruptly end after it became known the police were closing in on him. She would have an interesting encounter with Bundy in a bar only 90 minutes before he abducted Melissa Smith on October 18, 1974.

Louise Cannon walked into Widow McCoy's, a local bar in Salt Lake City, between 8:00 and 8:30 p.m. that 18th of October and passed Bundy as he was sipping a drink at the bar. As they spoke, she noticed he wasn't himself, so after exchanging the usual pleasantries, Louise went on to her table to meet her friends. And a few minutes later, Bundy slipped off the stool and walked out the door.

The full story of Louise Cannon's brief connection to Ted Bundy can be found in my book, *The Bundy Secrets: Hidden Files on America's Worst Serial Killer.*

Ted Bundy's rooming house at 565 First Avenue, Salt Lake City, Utah

Bundy lived in this upstairs apartment at 364 Douglas Avenue near the University of Utah law school. Courtesy Francine Bardole

CARLISLE, DR. AL

Dr. Al Carlisle (1937–2018) was the psychologist assigned to evaluate Ted Bundy after his conviction for the kidnapping of Carol DaRonch. Dr. Van O. Austin, prison psychiatrist, was involved with evaluating Ted Bundy as well, and the two men worked closely together to produce the most informative report possible. Both men concluded that Bundy was keeping aspects of himself hidden, which is so stated in their reports. It is also clear that Bundy liked and respected Al Carlisle, so much so, that after his recapture from his first escape in Colorado, he called him to discuss the circumstances of his escape. It should be noted from the recorded conversation that Ted Bundy was in a jovial mood as they discussed his ill-fated flight to freedom, and this is not the usual demeanor one detects from Bundy when listening to his other taped conversation of the authority figures with which Bundy was required to work.

CARTER, MIKE

Mike Carter is a veteran newspaperman with over 40 years' experience. Between 1974 – 1989, Carter worked for the Salt Lake Tribune, and as such his name heads up a number of articles about Bundy and the murders.

CASCADE MOUNTAINS

The Cascade Mountain range runs from British Columbia, through Washington State, into Oregon and northern California. A portion of the range is non-volcanic, while the northern section (including Washington State) is volcanic. For those well acquainted with the Ted Bundy murders, you'll know that Bundy made the Cascades famous by telling authorities that he dumped the remains of Donna Manson here. It is also reported that it's the location where Ted Bundy requested his ashes be scattered. However, no one has ever been able to confirm that the ashes were spread there or at any other location.

CENTRAL WASHINGTON STATE COLLEGE

Central Washington State College (now Central Washington University) lives large in the annals of the Ted Bundy murders. Located in Ellensburg, Washington, it was the site of the abduction of Susan Rancourt on April 17, 1974. Why Bundy chose this location at this time of the year is unknown. But his good friend, Terry Storwick, was attending the school at that time, and the possibility of being seen by him apparently didn't bother Bundy at all. Nevertheless, Bundy began hunting CWSC during the day and was seen around 2:00 p.m. by Kent Barnard as he passed the library, and he noticed he was wearing "a dark sling on his arm." Later that evening, Barnard and his girlfriend, Deanna, attended an anthropology class in Barge Hall, but he decided to leave early and walk over to the Arctic Circle; a location on campus where students often congregated. When he returned to Barge Hall before the class let out at 9:30, he again spotted the man with the sling on his arm standing in front of Barge Hall. He wasn't talking with anyone, Barnard said, and he believes he was smoking a cigarette with his right hand. The was the last time he saw Bundy. Within 30 minutes Bundy would encounter Susan Rancourt and he convinced her to help him, and she followed him to his car which was located in perhaps the most desolate location on campus. Bundy attacked her with a crowbar at the car, and after placing the unconscious woman in his VW (he had removed the passenger seat so he could lay her on the floor), he sped away from the campus. He would kill Susan Rancourt several miles away after exiting I-90 and driving up a deserted logging road.

CHAPMAN, DETECTIVE NORMAN

Detective Norman Chapman of the Pensacola Police Department would be forever linked to Ted Bundy after the killer's arrest on February 15, 1978. Brought into the station, Chapman would begin the initial questioning of the man who originally identified himself as one Kenneth Misner. Soon he'd be joined by Detective Don Patchen of the Tallahassee Police Department and Detective Steve Bodiford of the Leon County Sheriff's Department. And when it became clear Bundy was far more than a thief caught with many stolen credit cards, and became the prime suspect in the murders at Chi Omega, he was transferred to Tallahassee authorities.

CHEZ PIERRE

Chez Pierre was a posh French eatery in the city of Tallahassee, Florida that Bundy would frequent. While there, he purchased his meals with stolen credit cards.

CHI OMEGA

The Chi Omega Sorority house in Tallahassee, Florida, would gain national attention for the deadly attack upon its members in the early morning hours of January 15, 1978. Ted Bundy entered Chi Omega through an unlocked door a little before 3:00 a.m. He carried in his hand a log he'd picked up either on the outside of the sorority or nearby, and he immediately unleashed his pent-up homicidal rage. Four women, Margaret Bowman, Lisa Levy, Kathy Kleiner and Karen Chandler, would be savagely attacked. All the women would be beaten severely. Kathy Kleiner and Karen Chandler would survive with broken jaws, missing teeth, and would spend a very long time recovering from their injuries. Indeed, Kathy Kleiner told this author that she's had numerous operations over the years, the last being just a few years ago. Margaret Bowman and Lisa Levy would not be so lucky: both received a terrible bludgeoning (which may have caused their eventual deaths), but their cause of death was actually strangulation. Bundy would be forensically linked to the crime by the double bite mark he left on the buttocks of Lisa Levy.

CICCARELLI, DEBBIE

Debbie Ciccarelli, a Florida State University student, was living in a duplex at 431-B Dunwoody Street. Also living at 431-B was her friend, FSU student Nancy Young. Around 4:00 a.m., Debbie Ciccarelli was awakened by noises coming from 431-A, where their friend, Cheryl Thomas lived. Ciccarelli would later explain to a responding officer that she heard crying and a "loud, pounding noise coming from the apartment." As Ciccarelli and Young called out to their friend through the old thin walls of the duplex, they were only meant with silence. They also called her on the telephone but no one was answering. Oddly, they could hear the footsteps of someone walking around the apartment. After this, they called the police. And all the racket the young women were making saved Cheryl Thomas' life. Having beaten Thomas with the log he'd used at Chi Omega, Bundy was planning to strangle her while having sex with her from behind, but her neighbors forced him to scuttle his plans. After relieving himself through masturbation, Bundy went back out a rear window.

CLARK, DR. DONALD M.

Dr. Donald M. Clark, of Middleton, Colorado, performed the autopsy on Caryn Campbell, the nurse from Michigan who disappeared from the Wildwood Inn in Snowmass, Colorado on January 12, 1975. Her frozen and partially eaten body was located off Owl Creek Road on Monday, February 17, 1975, some 2.8 miles away from the Wildwood Inn.

CLECKLEY, HERVEY M.

Hervey M. Cleckley (1903-1984), was an American psychiatrist and author of the groundbreaking work, *The Mask of Sanity: An Attempt to Clarify Some Issues About the so-Called Psychopathic Personality*, originally published in 1941. Cleckley would also play a role in the Ted Bundy story. After Bundy's arrest in 1978 for the Chi Omega sorority murders, Emanuel Taney (see Taney, Emanuel this book) evaluated the accused for the defense and found him to be incompetent to stand trial. However, further testimony by Hervey Cleckley, whose book Taney used as a source to draw this conclusion, demonstrated that Ted Bundy was in fact competent to stand trial, and the trial went forward.

COLQUITT, SHARON

On February 8, 1978, Sharon Colquitt was working as a bartender at the Holiday Inn in Lake City, Florida. Sitting across from her on a bar stool was Ted Bundy who was talking with a man sitting next to him. It's clear Bundy made quite the impression of Colquitt, because despite that she was training another bartender, and the place was very busy with plenty of loud and distracting music, she remembered him well. And the biggest reason may be that Bundy had introduced himself as Mr. Evans (a name on a stolen credit card), but he signed the bar bill using the name Miller – from another stolen credit card in his possession.

CORSALETTI, LOU

Lou Corsaletti (1932-2002) was a much-beloved investigative reporter with *The Seattle Times*. In an obituary headline published in the paper on October 9, 2002, after stating Corsaletti's name and dates of birth and death, they wrote: "A newsman who always got it right. Corsaletti showed respect to everyone who came his way, and it's not surprising that he had friends everywhere." One friend said the following:

He was probably the last of the old-time police reporters — a decent human being who represented the very, very best in everything that's ethical in news today," said Redmond police Lt. Jim Taylor, a longtime source and personal friend. You could trust the guy, because he was more than just a reporter, he was a friend, and his word was as good as God's. I've known hundreds of reporters over the years, and if you ask me who was the best, I say Lou Corsaletti.

Of course, Corsaletti wrote many articles pertaining to the murders of the women of Washington state and beyond, and anyone researching the case will find his name attached to some of the best articles the paper had to offer.

COVEY, DUANE

Duane Covey was a University of Washington student and the last person to speak with Georgann Hawkins before she encountered Ted Bundy who was hobbling on crutches toward her in the alley behind Greek Row. The meeting itself was accidental, inasmuch as Georgann had been visiting her boyfriend in the same fraternity house where Covey lived, and when Covey heard the back-door slam shut, he poked his head out the window and called out to Georgann, and the two spoke for a couple of minutes. When their conversation ended, Duane turned away from the window and Georgann encountered Bundy within about one minute as she continued down the alley toward her sorority house.

COWART, JUDGE EDWARD

Judge Edward Cowart (1925–1987) was the presiding judge over the Chi Omega trial. And because the trial was televised nationwide, the entire country began to see what Floridians had known for years: Judge Cowart was not just a distinguished judge, but a witty all-around nice guy and those qualities were always on display. He was also respectful to Bundy in court, while at the same time, not tolerating any of his antics as the trial unfolded.

Once such incident occurred after Bundy had thrown a "temper tantrum" and was late to court. After he arrived, Cowart scolded him and warned him not to let it happen again or they would go on without him. At that point Bundy started shaking his index finger at the judge, and Cowart warned him to stop it immediately. Bundy then pointed his shaking finger at a Mr. Haggard, and Cowart told him that was alright. This particular encounter ended with a bit of humor when Bundy was giving a litany of injustices, he believed he was experiencing at the hands of the Leon County Jail officials. And when Bundy used the word "whoa" in his diatribe, Judge Cowart interrupted and said, "If you say "whoa" as it relates to these proceedings any more, I'm going to be using the spurs to overcome that." Bundy, who knew which way it was going and wanted to insert his own bit of humor, said "Giddyap, as it were." Cowart, never one to miss a beat, shot back: "Bless your heart. I just hope you'll stay with us, because if you don't, we'll miss you."

When Bundy was found guilty and subsequently sentenced to death in the electric chair, Judge Cowart is famous for speaking the following words to the convicted man: "Take care of yourself, young man. Take care of yourself. I say that to you sincerely. It's a tragedy to this court to see such a total waste of humanity. You're a bright young man. You'd have made a good lawyer. And I'd have loved to have you practice in front of me. I bear you no animosity, believe me. But you went the other way, partner. Take care of yourself."

COWELL, JACK

Jack Cowell was the uncle of Louise Cowell, Ted Bundy's mother. When Louise wanted to move across the county to Washington State, she chose to live for a time with her Uncle Jack. Even though their time living together under the same roof was not very long, Bundy grew to respect Jack Cowell, who, it has been reported was "an accomplished composer and pianist." Cowell was also a music professor at Puget Sound College. Later, Puget Sound College would become the University of Puget Sound.

COWELL, JOHN

John Cowell was Ted Bundy's cousin. He's mentioned in a number of places in the record, and what follows are two that are worthy of inclusion here:

Cousin: John Cowell lives at 719 N 3rd #202 Tacoma (corner of 3rd and N. Yakima) Works in Wash. Bldg at S. 11 and Pacific Ave in Tacoma. Vehicle Grey '67 Opel OYV 149

The Taylor Mountain area, 3.8 miles south of I-90 on Highway 18, was well known to Bundy. John Cowell, Bundy's cousin, used to hike with Ted east of Issaquah. On one occasion, they were driving in John's car on Highway 17 northbound. They drove slowly by the Bonneville power line road and Highway 18 (entrance to the crime scene), noticing the scenery. John's impression was that Ted may know the Highway 18 area very well. They used to drive through the area in 1972 and 1973.

COWELL, SAMUEL

Samuel Cowell was the father of Louise Cowell and the grandfather of Ted Bundy. In the annals of Bundy, Sam Cowell does not fare well. There were rumors of Cowell being an angry man and one that was sometime violent. People often point the finger at Samuel Cowell as having had a collection of pornography that Bundy would occasionally "raid." and that he could be found addressing imaginary beings in the home. Lastly, some have put forth the rumor that Sam Cowell may have been the father of Ted Bundy, which, if true, would top the list of salacious and depraved acts committed by Sam Cowell. Of course, these are but rumors, and as far as this author knows, the incest charge is without foundation. Bundy, for his part, always looked up to his well-educated grandfather, and stated he only had fond memories of the man.

CULVER, LYNETTE

Lynette Culver (1962–1975), 12, was attending Alameda Junior High in Pocatello, Idaho when she disappeared from the school at lunchtime om May 6, 1975. Bundy, who had come to Pocatello the day before to hunt college women at the university but failed to obtain one, would find what he was looking for the following day. Bundy left the Holiday Inn (but did not check out) started trolling, and happened upon the school at the time many students were leaving for lunch.

As he pulled his VW up to the curb directly in front of the school, he spotted young Lynette Culver and motioned him over to his car. For reasons unknown, Bundy convinced her to get into his vehicle and the two drove away from the school. It is unknown whether Bundy crashed a crowbar into the rear portion of Lynette's head as he drove, and then headed back to his first-floor room in the rear of the Holiday Inn, or if he actually convinced her to enter his room under her own strength before attacking her. What is known is that Ted Bundy admitted to drowning the young girl in the bathtub, and then afterward, he said he had sex with her dead body. Bundy would, in an hour or two, pack up his belongings and perhaps with the help of a blanket, quickly move the deceased girl to his trunk of his car which was located in the front of the vehicle. Bundy would tell authorities during his last confessions, that he slid her into a river about five miles north of Pocatello. That river was the Snake River.

Alameda Middle School, Pocatello, Idaho

The rear portion of the Holiday Inn in Pocatello, Idaho

CUNNINGHAM, JULIE

On March 15, 1975, Julie Cunningham (1949-1975) would encounter Ted Bundy while he was seeking a victim in Vail, Colorado. Once again, Bundy was hunting in a famous and popular ski resort town in his attempt to duplicate the same success he'd had when he snatched Caryn Campbell from the Wildwood Inn in Snowmass, Colorado. And once again, he would not be denied. Around 9:00 p.m., Bundy, hobbling on crutches while holding ski boots, was making his way up a Vail street lined with nice shops on both sides of the street. He kept his eyes looking ahead for any potential victims who might see him struggling and offer help. After just a moment he noticed a blond woman who had also spotted him. That woman was Julie Cunningham, 26, a resident of Vail who was even then making her way to a bar to have drinks and perhaps some dinner with a friend. But because she could see that Bundy was having such a difficult time fumbling with the boots while using the crutches, she offered to help him. And as they made the rather long walk to his car and they were talking, she mentioned her plans for the evening to Bundy and made a remark that she'd be running late.

Upon reaching the car, Julie, in that last normal moment of her life, was attempting to place the boots in Bundy's VW when her killer reached down and picked up the crowbar he placed behind the vehicle (just as he had done in the Georgann Hawkins abduction), and struck her very hard on her head knocking her out cold. Bundy quickly heaves her into his vehicle, jumps in the driver's seat and quickly places handcuffs on her. From here he made his way to a rural area near Rifle, Colorado, some 90 miles west of Vail. Once he located a spot where he was comfortable stopping, he did so, and over a short period he raped her and strangled her back into unconsciousness. Leaving the car for a few minutes (he left the passenger side door open intentionally), she came to, jumped out of the car and started running and screaming into the darkness. Bundy allowed her to run for a moment before he chased her down and strangled her to death. He pulled the body up a hillside and left it there. By April 4th, however, he was back in Colorado to bury her, and he was surprised to find her untouched by the wildlife. He also remarked that her body looked mummified which it's clear he didn't expect. After her burial, he sought out another victim, and that victim would be Denise Oliverson of Grand Junction, Colorado.

CURTIS, JANE

Jane Curtis, 21, was a student at Central Washington State College, and came very close to becoming a Ted Bundy victim. This, of course, is the same college where Susan Rancourt was abducted by Ted Bundy on April 17, 1974. After her abduction, Curtis came to the authorities to tell her story of the strange man with his arm in a sling that she helped carry books to his car on a Sunday evening. She wasn't certain of the date, but it was either the Sunday before Wednesday the 17th, or the following Sunday. In any event, Curtis said she was in Bouillon Library and had been stacking books for a couple of hours. Between 8:30 and 9:00 p.m., she left the library and exited the front doors, which were the only doors where students were allowed to enter or exit the building. Within moments of coming outside, she noticed a man with his arm in a cast (she told detectives it wasn't a hard cast, but more like gauze wrapped around the arm) attempting to carry eight or nine heavy hardbound books.

Of course, this would draw attention and Bundy was counting on it. Not only that, but he immediately dropped them, and being a normal person, Jane Curtis offered to help. Curtis assumed he was going to the parking lot directly behind and across the small street from the library. So when they crossed the little bridge that goes over the man-made pond (which sits between Bouillon Library and the Group Conference Center), instead of walking straight, or angling right to the main parking lot that is directly behind the library and across the narrow street, he started walking to the left, toward a darker and more isolated area of the campus where his car was parked by a railroad trestle that was bounded by tall grass. Curtis said that he stayed to her left as they walked, and she caught him turning his head to look at her and when she looked at him, she noticed how weird his eyes were (apparently his eyes were fine as they first spoke minutes earlier, but as the actual attack neared, they began to exhibit a type of neurotransmitter change, which caused her to take notice).

As they were nearing the car, he began to complain about the pain in his arm. He asked her to open the car but she refused – she was, after all, carrying most of the heavy books. When Bundy did unlock the passenger side door and open it, Curtis was troubled by what she saw: the passenger seat was out and she was looking at the flat surface of the car floor where the seat should be. At that point the man told her to get into the car but she again refused. He explained that because his arm was hurting, he just wanted her to start the car for him. None of this mattered to Jane Curtis, and within seconds she quickly got away from him.

CURTIS, SUSAN

Susan Curtis (1960-1975) was 15 years-old when she became a victim of Ted Bundy on June 27, 1975, while attending a youth conference at Brigham Young University in Provo, Utah. Susan had just finished dinner in the Wilkinson Student Center, when she headed out into what one newspaper described as the "fading light." Desiring to take care of her teeth (she had braces) she was returning to her room so she could brush them, and she'd told a friend she'd be back in a few minutes. She was never seen again.

Only minutes before his execution on January 24, 1989, Ted Bundy would admit to her murder but gave no details.

DANTE'S TAVERN

Dante's Tavern at 5300 Roosevelt Road, Seattle, Washington

Dante's Tavern, located at 5300 Roosevelt Way N.E., was a bar that Ted Bundy would occasionally visit. It was likely he was there on the evening of January 31, 1974 and spotted Lynda Ann Healy and her three friends sharing a pitcher of beer at a nearby table. It is also fairly certain that once the foursome decided to leave, he followed them to the rooming house where Healy and her friend lived only several blocks away. Within minutes of the four going back inside the home, their male friend, Pete Neil, came out and hurried to the bus stop to catch the 941 back to his place. Bundy had to have witnessed this. And a little later he would go up the front steps and try the front door to see of it was unlocked, and it was. He had no intention of entering just yet. He'd wait, he reasoned, until well after midnight before exploring the inside of the house, and abducting a victim. That victim was Lynda Ann Healy.

DARONCH, CAROL

In 1974, Carol DaRonch, 18, was employed by Mountain Bell telephone company in Salt Lake City, Utah. When Carol clocked out from work on Friday, November 8, 1974, she headed home but would not be there long, as she wanted to drive over to the Fashion Place Mall in Murray, Utah, so that she could purchase a Christmas present. While there, a man came up to her and introduced himself as "Officer Roseland." Bundy was now playing cop. He told Carol that someone had attempted to break into her car, and would she please follow him out to it. She did so, but all looked well after viewing it. Oddly, Bundy wanted her to get into her car and take a better look, but Carol refused. Bundy and Carol then walked back through the mall and across the side street on the other side of the mall where Bundy said his partner was holding a suspect in a police substation. However, that building was a cleaners and when Bundy tried to open a side door marked 139, it was locked; something he already knew. He then said he needed to take her to the main Murray, Utah Police Department, and so they walked the twenty or so feet to his VW Bug. Carol, expecting him to drive straight ahead to State Street and on to the police station, was surprised to see Bundy twirl the steering wheel to the left and quickly make a U-turn. Within moments, he turned left again and a minute or so later, stopped abruptly in front of the McMillan Elementary school and attacked her. However, Carol fought hard to get away, and because Bundy had gotten both handcuffs on her right wrist, Carol DaRonch was able to get out of the car and start running away. The next moment she saw car lights coming toward her, and an older couple stopped and picked up the distraught young woman and drove her to the police station. Bundy quickly drove away. Carol DaRonch is the only verifiable victim known to have escaped Ted Bundy.

The building across the side street from the fashion Place Mall. It would be here that Bundy led Carol DaRonch by falsely telling her it was a police substation.

This is the location of the McMillan Elementary School in Murray, Utah where Bundy attacked Carol DaRonch after stopping his VW in this bus drop-off lane in front of the school.

DAVIS, ROSS

In May of 1973, Ted Bundy went to work with for Ross Davis at the Republican State Central Committee in Olympia, Washington. Although Davis was his boss, the two men became friends, and Bundy even spent time at the Davis home and got to know the family very well. During that summer, Bundy was promoted to Davis' assistant. He would leave that position at the end of summer so that he could attend the law school at the University of Puget Sound. Later, when Bundy was being looked at as a possible killer of women, Davis, like all those who knew and liked Bundy, had a difficult time believing it. Indeed, while they would all finally "get there," if you will, it's a reality that would only happen over time, as the circumstantial kept adding up that Bundy was in fact the killer of all these women.

DAWES, DEPUTY KEITH

On February 11, 1978, Leon County Sheriff's Deputy, Keith Dawes, spotted Bundy around 1:00 a.m. as he was standing next a 1975 Toyota sedan, he'd stolen some eight hours earlier. Dawes, for his part, wisely decided to see what this individual was doing out so late at night standing around parked cars. Seeing Dawes' patrol car pull up, and then having him walk up to him, must have sent Bundy's heart racing. When the officer asked Bundy for identification, he had to admit he didn't have any. Dawes then inquired as to where he lived. "College Avenue" Bundy blurted out without thinking about it. College Avenue was only one block over from where they were standing.

When Dawes shined his flashlight into the car, he spotted a license plate and Bundy quickly made the excuse that he'd found it but didn't know what to do with it. As he handed the plate off to Dawes, he knew escape was his only answer. As Deputy Dawes retraced his steps to run the plate as well as the Toyota's, Bundy, like a gazelle, took off down the street, which confirmed to the officer that he had indeed made the right decision to question him. That license plate that came from inside the car was the same one that was used on the FSU media van that Bundy used on his trip to Jacksonville, where he attempted to abduct 14 year-old Leslie Parmenter, whose brother not only saved her from being abducted, but had scribbled down the license number as well (both Parmenters would later identify Bundy as the man driving the white van that day). Dawes quickly discovered the sedan was stolen and he had it towed. He too would later identify Ted Bundy as the one he was questioning in those early morning hours.

DAWSON, DR. PAUL

Dr. Paul Dawson, a psychologist, claims to have interviewed Ted Bundy while he was in prison, and is the author of the book, *Faces of Ted Bundy: My Prison Interviews of Bundy*.

DEKLE, BOB

Bob Dekle was the lead prosecutor in the Kimberly Diane Leach murder trial, which resulted in a conviction of Ted Bundy, and ultimately, a sentence of death. That sentence was carried out, despite several failed appeals, on January 24, 1989. He recently stated on a documentary about the case, that he wished Bundy could have been brought back after his execution so he could execute him again, and keep repeating the process for about 30 times. His book, *The Last Murder*, tells the story of the murder, the intense investigation that followed, and the trial that cost Bundy his life.

DENVER, COLORADO

Denver, Colorado plays a part in the Ted Bundy story, inasmuch that Bundy killed in the state and may have gone through the city on one or more occasions. That said, it appears he didn't abduct anyone from that city, and he may not have hunted the women and young girls of Denver at all. However, the CBI (Colorado Bureau of Investigation) was in the city, and it would be here that Detective Michael Fisher would bring Ted Bundy's VW (having borrowed it from Utah authorities), to search for additional evidence. Fisher's decision to do so was confirmed correct when CBI officials discovered the additional evidence of blood that had run down the passenger side window, passed the weather felt, and down into the internal area of the door. Also discovered were additional hairs from some of the victims, as well as strands of head hair from almost-victim, Carol DaRonch.

DICKEY, OFFICER ROY

Officer Roy Dickey, of the Tallahassee Police Department would spot a suspicious suspect in the late afternoon of February 10, 1978. What follows is from my book, *The Bundy Murders*:

On that same evening, Tallahassee Officer Roy Dickey was sitting in his unmarked car on the south side of West St. Augustine Street, where it meets Dunwoody Street to, as he would later write, "observe any late night-early morning activity which might yield information relating to the Chi-omega murder 1-15-78." St. Augustine is a one-way street heading east, which meant Officer Dickey was facing east with his back toward Stadium Drive. At approximately 10:45 p.m., Bundy was walking north on Stadium Drive, and just as he rounded the corner onto West St. Augustine, Roy Dickey noticed him. Bundy spotted the officer right away too, as noted in Dickey's report, which says the individual took evasive action by quickly walking between two houses in an attempt to get to Pensacola Avenue, one block north. As soon as Dickey saw what Bundy was doing, he radioed Officer Donald Porter, who was stationed in his vehicle at Pensacola and Woodward, just a short distance east of where Bundy should have come out, but didn't. Despite the efforts of both officers, Bundy was not seen again; but later, Officer Dickey would positively identify him as the man he saw disappear between the two houses that night.

DOBSON, DR. JAMES

Dr. James Dobson, at Ted Bundy request, was granted the last media interview on January 23, 1989, and less than 24 hours before the killer's death. For many who knew Bundy, it was considered an odd choice, and in fact, once the interview was aired from coast to coast here in the United States (as well as being picked up by foreign media), it became clear as to why Dobson had been given the interview in the first place. In the interview, Bundy begins blaming pornography for the reason he became a killer of women. This was seen by many to be absurd, and was quickly rebutted by experts in the field, including Dr, Emanuel Tanay, who had interviewed Bundy previously for his defense team in Florida. Tanay said the following about Bundy's pornography claim, as noted in an Orlando Sentinel article, published on January 26, 1989:

That's one more of his manipulations. Pornography doesn't have the power to cause the severe deformity of personality that he had.

DODGE, WARREN

Warren Dodge was one of two of Bundy's very good friends that he had as they were growing up. And in what might have been a good point of humor and discussion between the two boys, was the fact that Dodge and Bundy were born on the same day, with Warren drawing his first breath twenty minutes before Bundy. In a July 3, 1986 article in the *Tacoma News Tribune,* Dodge speaks of a Bundy he knew that was unlike the one that was sitting on death row. Like many, he couldn't bring himself to believe his good friend could be involved with the murders: "Originally, I couldn't imagine he did any of those things." Over time, however, he came to understand Bundy was the one responsible. Even so, he didn't want to think in terms of Bundy being executed. He understood his friend could never be free again, but he preferred him to be alive.

The last time the two men saw each other was in 1972 when Bundy stopped to help them move, and they all had a few beers. But it was in 1975, after Bundy had been arrested in Utah, and the world was starting to wonder about him and his possible connection to the murders, that Bundy chose to stop by for a visit. What follows is from that 1986 article:

Later, while out on bail... Bundy showed up at Dodge's doorstep one day while Dodge's wife was home: 'Her only reaction was absolute fear. She would not allow him in the home. She talked to him on the porch a while. She tried as best she could to make him go away'.

The article goes on to say that she told Bundy Warren would be home the next day, but he never returned.

D'OLIVO, KATHLEEN

Kathleen D'Olivo, like Jane Curtis, also had an encounter with Ted Bundy at Central Washington State College, but it was on Wednesday April 17, 1974, and only about two hours before Susan Rancourt succumbed to his wiles.

On this night, D'Olivo arrived at the Bouillon Library around 8:00 p.m. and spent the next two hours studying on the second floor in the curriculum laboratory. At 10:00 p.m., she closed her books and prepared to leave. It was her custom to telephone her fiancé at that time and she didn't want to be late. Like all students, she left the library through the front door, turned right and was making her way back to her car that was parked in the lot directly behind and across the street from Bouillon Library. It was at this time she heard the dropping of heavy books. What follows is taken directly from her statement to King County Police:

KATHLEEN: *I walked out, I took a right, which was leading across the front part of the library, cement porch-like, whatever, and was cutting across a lawn that went between the library and Black Hall. I was aiming toward the parking lot where the car was parked. I hadn't quite gotten off the lawn, or sidewalk. Wherever I was, I hadn't reached the main mall stretch when I heard something behind me. It sounded like something following me, it didn't startle me or anything, it wasn't a loud noise and I turned around and there was a man dropping books, he was squatting, he was trying to pick up the books and packages was what he was doing, and so I noticed that he had a sling on one arm, and a hand brace on the other. I didn't really notice it at the time, I just noticed that he was unable to pick up that many things and I assumed that he was going to the library. I went over and said, "Do you need some help?" He said, "Yeah, could you?" or something to that affect. So I picked up what was to me felt like a bicycle backpack, it was light nylon material, kind of.*

At this time Bundy knew his ruse was working and as far as he was concerned, she was as good as his. All he had to do was maintain a calm and composed attitude as well as keeping an eye out for any problems that might crop up along the way. Kathleen didn't yet know it, but he was taking her to what was arguably the most isolated location on campus. She's then asked to describe the packages the man was carrying and she elaborated. Continuing with her statement:

KATHLEEN: *Yes. Some packages, three boxes that were small, not large. I think they were wrapped in parcel post, or brown paper bag-type thing and I think some of them had string ties on them, you know, like ... I'm almost sure on that, but at any rate, I picked up the bag that I thought had books in it, the knapsack type bag, and he picked up the packages.*

When Kathleen offered help, she believed she was helping him to take his books and packages into the library. But when she noticed he was heading to the small bridge which leads away from the library, she asked him what they were doing. At that point Bundy said he was going to his car and motioned in the direction it was parked. Confident she could handle the situation if the injured man tried anything, they continued walking to the car. She would watch him closely. Kathleen describes what happened once they reached the car:

KATHLEEN: I set the pack down, well first of all, he went to unlock the door on the passenger side, which is the inside... I mean, the car was parked right next to a log and there was room between it for a person, and he went to unlock the car on the passenger's side, and I set down the package (the pack) that I had been carrying and leaned it against the log and I think I said goodbye... anyways, my thought was well, I had done my deed and I was going to leave, and then he was supposedly unlocking the car and he dropped the key; then he felt for the key with his right hand and he couldn't find it apparently and he said, "Do you think you could find it for me because I can't feel with this thing on my hand (meaning the brace on his right hand). I was cautious at this time, I mean, even while we were walking, I thought well, I'm not going to let him get behind me, I'm gonna keep an eye on him, I've got these heavy books and I can use them. But I didn't want to bend over in front of him so I said, let's step back and see if we can see the reflection in the light, so we stepped back behind the car, kind of behind the car to the side, and I squatted down and luckily I did see the reflection of the key in the light so I picked up the key and dropped them in his hand and I said goodbye and good luck, or something with your arm, or something to that affect, and that was the end of the conversation.

Kathleen D'Olivo believes he said "Thank you" as she walked away.

DOROS, JAMES

James Doros was a housemate of Ted Bundy in 1974, when they both lived in the Rogers rooming house in Seattle. Living in a basement apartment, Doros got to know Bundy very well, and, when interviewed, would tell police of Bundy's odd speech pattern and accent, stating it, "as having a clipped, concise diction pattern similar to an Englishman who had been Americanized."

DOWDY, NANCY

Nancy Dowdy was a member of the Chi Omega Sorority and the roommate of Nita Neary. In the early morning hours of January 15, 1978, Neary came through the rear door of the sorority house, and just before she reached the staircase that would take her upstairs to her room, she saw a man dressed in a coat and cap heading down the stairs. Standing very still in the darkness, the man never saw her, and she noticed he was carrying a club in his hand. Once he walked out the front door, Neary went up to her room and awakened Nancy Dowdy and the two women went downstairs to see if everything was alright. Returning upstairs, the two women awakened house president, Jackie McGill. While McGill was trying to take it all in, Karen Chandler came stumbling out of room 8 holding her bloodied head.

DUNN, DETECTIVE ROGER

Detective Roger Dunn, of the King County Police (and partner of Detective Robert D. Keppel), had an interesting meeting/exchange with Bundy one morning after he and Bob Keppel caught up with the killer as he was walking back into Marlin and Sheila Vortman's apartment (the couple was not at home at the time) in Washington State. What follows is from Detective Dunn's report:

I pulled up to him as he was walking back toward the apartment house, (I) got out of the car and identified myself. He asked if I had a subpoena or a warrant and I told him that I didn't. I said I (would) just like to talk to him and he said well come on inside and I'll see what we can do."

As soon as Dunn and Bundy were in the apartment, Bundy telephoned his attorney, John Browne but he was not yet in the office, so he explained the situation and told them to tell Browne to call as soon as possible. Within minutes Browne called and asked Bundy if Dunn was still in the apartment. As can be expected, their meeting ended immediately. However, as Dunn was leaving, Bundy said something rather cryptic, the meaning of which was not lost on Dunn. Again, from Dunn's report:

Bundy said that he would really like to help out because of all the pressure that was on us from the press and said that he felt no pressure... I emphasized that we would like to eliminate him if we could but had so far been unable to. He said that there were things he knew that we didn't know but that he didn't feel at liberty to discuss them.

ELIZABETH LUND HOME FOR UNWED MOTHERS

Ted Bundy was born at the Elizabeth Lund Home for Unwed Mothers, in Burlington, Vermont, on November 24, 1946. His mother, Louise Cowell, due to the "acceptable norms" of that time, traveled from her home in Philadelphia to have the child in Vermont, and she entered the home in her seventh month of pregnancy. She would spend sixty-three days there before returning to her parents' Pennsylvania home.

ELLENSBURG, WASHINGTON

Ellensburg, Washington plays a part in the Ted Bundy story through the town's connection with Central Washington State College, where Susan Rancourt was abducted by Ted Bundy on Wednesday, April 17, 1974.

ELLIS, MEGAN

Megan Ellis was a friend of Donna Manson, as the two were students at Evergreen State College in Olympia, Washington. Manson would disappear on her way to a jazz concert being held at the library on March 12, 1974. At first, Megan didn't see her absence as a cause of concern; however, when she still had not been seen a week later, Megan contacted the university police and filled out a missing person's report.

ELWAY, STUART

Stuart Elway and Ted Bundy were friends and fellow Republicans who had waged political campaigns together. They hit it off so well, that at one time they considered getting an apartment together. As can be expected, it hit Elway hard when he finally realized that his friend was in fact the killer of the women in the Pacific Northwest and beyond. It was a shock that was common place to those who knew and liked Bundy, as they never saw anything in his life that could point to him being a murderer.

ERICKSON, CHUCK

Chuck Erickson was the chief probation and parole officer whose office was located in the Pitkin County courthouse in Aspen where Ted Bundy was being housed in the jail there, while he awaited (and then participated in) his trial for the murder of Caryn Campbell whom he abducted from the

Wildwood Inn on March 15, 1975. Campbell was murdered within three hours of being abducted (per autopsy results), and probably much earlier. What follows is from *The Trail of Ted Bundy: Digging Up the Untold Stories*, and the remainder of Erickson's story can be found there.

Chuck Erickson, chief probation and parole officer at the jail, had an office on the second floor. During a telephone conversation on November 7, 2015, he explained how the guards would bring Bundy by elevator to the second floor so that he could use the law library, and there was no mistaking the sound of shuffling leg irons. When the sound of the jangling began, everyone knew Ted Bundy was coming down the hall. From where his office was located, Erickson said he could hear Bundy approaching but couldn't see him as he passed the open door. His secretary, Sandra Yates (a pseudonym), would hear the rattling of the chains as well, and for her, it was a sound she could do without. She didn't like seeing Bundy and she always avoided, she said, looking directly into his eyes.

Erickson, who spoke with Bundy probably a half-dozen times as he passed his cell, said the prisoner was always nice and polite, and the probation and parole officer mentioned he'd loaned Bundy a "criminal justice" type board game, because the prisoner had complained of boredom. But the game, Erickson said with a laugh, was always placing Bundy back in jail! Bundy, however, was more than just about board games, and even after his disastrous first attempt at freedom, he was determined to do it again. After he rested and regained his strength, he would again find a way to escape.

EVANS, GOVERNOR DAN

In September 1972, Bundy became part of the re-elect team for Governor Dan Evans. Although it was an unpaid position, Bundy threw himself into the work, and his main thrust was to spy on the governor's challenger, Albert Rosellini, and report back with any pertinent info he obtained. Rosellini, a two-time governor of the state (1957-1965) would be soundly defeated by Governor Evans the following year.

EVERGREEN STATE COLLEGE

Evergreen State College, located in Olympia, Washington, was the site of the abduction of Donna Manson, on March 12, 1974 (see full story under Manson, Donna). The college has a unique, almost rustic appeal, seeing that it was carved out of and constructed in the midst of a forest of fir trees. Many of the buildings are concrete bunker-like structures that, in my opinion, match perfectly with its surroundings. And one aspect that did not go unnoticed by Bundy was the numerous winding foot paths that traverse the school, almost all of which are encased by trees.

EVERITT, RANDY

Randy Everitt was an investigator with the Idaho Attorney General's Office, and participated, along with Chief Idaho Investigator Russell Reneau, in the final confession of Ted Bundy. Bundy had committed two murders in the state, and the two investigators had but one hour to interview Bundy. Present also (per Bundy's wishes) were his attorney, Dianna Weiner, and FBI agent Bill Hagmaier of the Behavioral Science Unit. During that hour, the investigators jumped back and forth between the two murders, and at one point when they asked Bundy the manner of death for Lynette Culver, he said drowning. And because Bundy had already mentioned that he placed her body into a river five miles north of Pocatello, they temporarily assumed she drowned in the river. However, as they were leaving the prison, Reneau, realizing that Bundy never made the drowning clear, asked

Everitt to go back into the prison and see if he could speak to Bundy one more time. Once inside, they led Randy Everitt into a room where he waited about 20 minutes until Bundy was led into the room. Sitting in chairs facing each other, perhaps through glass, Everitt questioned Bundy as to how she drowned. Bundy, almost as if it was an afterthought, responded that he placed her in the bathtub of his room at the Holiday Inn and drowned her. This testimony did not come out in the recorded one-hour session that was later transcribed featuring Bundy's official confession that was attended by Bundy, Reneau, Everitt, Hagmaier, and Weiner. As such, the news of how Culver was actually killed remained relatively unknown until this information was confirmed and published in my book, *The Bundy Murders: A Comprehensive History.*

FARGO, LORRAINE

Lorraine Fargo was the last person to speak with Kathy Parks before she disappeared from Oregon State University on May 6, 1974. Bundy would later say he drove the 250 miles south to Corvallis, Oregon to throw off the Seattle authorities. Bundy, who loved hunting women in the university setting, would get in and out of OSU without ever being noticed, and he would leave with what he came for: a victim.

On this night, Lorraine Fargo had been studying at the library and would run into Kathy Parks around 10:30 p.m. as she was heading to the Memorial Union Commons cafeteria, which, by the way, was getting ready to close by 11:00 p.m. When the two women met, they stood and talked on the sidewalk just across the narrow street from the Memorial Union Commons, and it's likely Bundy was watching them (read the full story of their encounter in Lorraine's own words in my book, *The Trail of Ted Bundy: Digging Up the Untold Stories*).

Because Kathy was having boyfriend problems, Lorraine invited her to come back to their dorm in Sackett Hall and talk, but Kathy said she just needed to walk a while and that she'd come over later. After they said their goodbyes, Lorraine continued her walk to Sackett Hall while Kathy crossed the small street and ascended the steps that led to the cafeteria at the Commons. Soon after this, Bundy would introduce himself to her in the cafeteria, and by some type of ruse, would convince Kathy to leave with him. Once they were beyond the eyes and reach of other humans, Bundy took control of her and transported her back to Washington State where he killed her. A portion of her remains (her skull) was later discovered with the partial remains (skulls, mandibles, etc.) of others, on Taylor Mountain.

On the evening of May 6, 1974, Kathy Parks and Lorraine Fargo, both Oregon State University students, spent a few minutes talking on the sidewalk area seen in the above photo. Afterward, Kathy crossed the small street and entered the Memorial Union Commons by way of the steps seen on the right; the steps being partly obscured by the street light. Minutes later, Ted Bundy introduced himself to Kathy and convinced her to leave with him.

FARMER, MILLARD

Millard Farmer was an attorney based in Atlanta, Georgia, that would play an advisory role for Bundy, and would assist Mike Minerva and his Public Defender's team, in their attempt to save the killer's life. Farmer was unable to assist in an official capacity due to a prior legal snag that prevented him from practicing in Florida. Yet no one, not even Millard Farmer, could talk any sense into Bundy, and his lack of heeding their warnings would cost Bundy his life.

FERRIS, SYBIL

Sybil Ferris was an older woman who befriended Ted Bundy, and Bundy, true to form, would take advantage of her. Some of the things that bothered her about Bundy was his borrowing money and then making excuses as to why he couldn't pay it back, borrowing her car and not returning it on time, as well as other classic Bundy habits of taking or using, and feeling no responsibility to pay back or make things right. Even so, Ferris was also a very astute person and was able to put things together in her head as to what Ted Bundy might really be. A nurse who was trained to recognize psychological traits in individuals, was seeing Ted Bundy for what he was. What follows is from Dr. Carlisle's book, *Violent Mind: The 1976 Psychological Assessment of Ted Bundy*:

I have been suspicious from the day those two girls were killed at Lake Sammamish with that "Ted." I remember seeing him in an Albertson's store in Green Lake with a cast on his arm. I was going to do something about it, but living alone I was afraid to do more than what I had already done.

When Carlisle asked her if Bundy seemed strange, mentally ill, or a criminal, she said: *"He seemed to have mental problems, although I couldn't place him in any diagnostic category."*

No matter the category, Sybil Ferris was right on target as to her suspicions of Ted Bundy, and unlike many others, his exposure as a killer of women did not surprise her at all.

FIFE, OFFICER JOHN

Officer John Fife, of the Salt Lake County Sheriff's Office, was one of the responding patrolmen when Ted Bundy was stopped and placed under arrest by Sergeant Bob Hayward of the Utah Highway Patrol, in the early morning hours of August 16, 1975. This arrest would lead to the unveiling of who and what Ted Bundy actually was.

FILMS

What follows are American films on Ted Bundy, the year they were released, and the stars who played Bundy:
The Deliberate Stranger (1986) Mark Harmon
Ted Bundy (2002) Michael Reilly Burke
The Stranger Beside Me (2003) Billy Campbell
The Riverman (2004) Cary Elwes
Bundy: A Legacy of Evil (2008) Corin Nemec
The Capture of the Green River Killer (James Marsters)
Extremely Wicked, Shockingly Evil and Vile (2019) Zac Efron

FISHER, DETECTIVE MICHAEL

Detective Michael Fisher was the chief criminal investigator for the Ninth Judicial District, State of Colorado, with an office based in Glenwood Springs, Colorado. Fisher's entrance into the Bundy case came when he was summoned to investigate the disappearance of one Caryn Campbell who vanished from the Wildwood Inn in Snowmass, Colorado on January 12, 1975. Campbell, a nurse from Michigan, had come to a medical conference with her boyfriend, Doctor Raymond Gadowski and his two children. They were also accompanied by a Doctor Rosenthall, who also happened to be a former boyfriend of Caryn. Doctors Gadowski and Rosenthall were quickly ruled out as likely suspects.

The investigation into the disappearance of Caryn Campbell (and within weeks her murder, after her body was discovered less than three miles away from the inn) would occupy the life of Detective Fisher for the next 15 years. And as Theodore Robert Bundy surfaced as the sole suspect, through tireless efforts and dogged determination, Fisher would succeed in getting the first murder warrant placed against Bundy for Campbell's murder. Towards the end of Bundy's life, Mike Fisher, along with fellow Colorado investigator, Matt Lindvall, would hear the killer's confessions concerning those he had murdered in the state.

FLETCHER, ART

Art Fletcher (1924–2005) was a Republican political figure in Washington State politics. In 1968, Fletcher ran for the office of Lieutenant Governor of Washington State, but he failed to unseat the incumbent, John Cherberg. Ted Bundy, who had been asked to join the campaign, did so, and ultimately became Fletcher's personal driver. Fletcher, an army veteran of the Second World War, is buried in Arlington National Cemetery.

FONIS, DETECTIVE TED

Seattle Police Detective Ted Fonis (1922–2011), badge #1393, worked closely with Robert Keppel and his team from the King County Police. Indeed, after Ted Bundy exploded on the radar of law enforcement after he was charged in the kidnapping of Carol DaRonch in Utah, Keppel and Fonis travelled together to Salt Lake City to learn about Bundy's activities there and to compare the cases Washington had with those of Utah. What follows is from *The Bundy Murders: A Comprehensive History:*

Even while the Ted-weary citizens of Washington were sipping their first cup of coffee for the day and mulling over the wall of denial Captain Mackie was building, detectives Robert Keppel and Ted Fonis were hopping a United Airlines flight to Utah. Keppel telephoned Jerry Thompson to set up a meeting even before heading to their hotel, where Thompson soon met them. Here the three investigators discussed the murders and Ted Bundy in detail, and it appeared to the Seattle pair that Utah had a good case against him.

It would be a long but productive day for the trio of lawmen. Homicide reports, missing persons reports, autopsy reports, and other investigative reports were retrieved from metal file cabinets, viewed and copied. Photographs of the decedents from Utah and Colorado were studied with respect to the damage done to the skulls of the young women. The similarities to their Washington counterparts were noted. While in Murray (where Bundy's fate ultimately rested), Thompson gave the detectives a tour of the Fashion Place Mall and drove the men along the same route Bundy had taken with Carol DaRonch to the McMillan School where he attacked her. Thompson also filled them in on the details of the Kent abduction and the ongoing investigation in Bountiful.

FORBES, DETECTIVE BEN

Originally from Scotland, Detective Ben Forbes (1936-1991) was a homicide investigator with the Salt Lake County Sheriff's Office in Salt Lake City, Utah. His partner, Detective Jerry Thompson, was the lead investigator for the Bundy case in Utah.

When Bundy was arrested in the early morning hours of August 16, 1975 and was booked on the charge of evading a police officer, he no doubt believed he didn't have a great deal to worry about. However, five days later, Bundy was arrested for the second time and hauled off to jail. This time he was charged with possession of burglary tools.

Of course, the implements he carried in a gym bag: rope, an electrical cord, ski mask, ice pick, strips of cloth torn from a bedsheet, and other items were not being used to break into houses, but were a part of his murder kit. Unbeknownst to Bundy, the detectives from the get-go believed Bundy was far more than a burglar. And Forbes is famous for startling Bundy with this revelation during an interview at police headquarters around 6:00 p.m. that August 21, 1975. Discussing the various items Bundy had in his kit, Forbes suddenly blurted out: "My game is homicide!" This dramatic outburst told Bundy everything he needed to hear as to the direction the police were going.

GADOWSKI, DR. RAYMOND

Dr. Raymond Gadowski was the boyfriend of Caryn Campbell (both from Michigan), who disappeared from the Wildwood Inn in Snowmass, Colorado. The circumstances surrounding her disappearance/abduction are inexorably linked to the events just preceding the event that would cause her to lose her life. On the evening of January 12, 1975, Dr. Gadowski, Caryn, Dr. Rosenthall, and the two Gadowski children, had dinner at the Stew Pot, located in Snowmass Village.

Because Caryn wasn't feeling well, she ordered stew with a glass of milk, but did not finish either. After a quick stop to look at magazines at a shop, they walked back to the inn. Caryn had agreed to trade a *Viva* (Viva, published 1973-1980, was basically an erotic magazine for women) for Dr. Rosenthall's *Playboy*. Now here is where the "what ifs" begin to rise as we see what could have happened to alter her fate.

As they entered the Wildwood Inn, Caryn asked Raymond to get the magazine from their room, but he demurred saying he wanted to sit in a chair around the fire in the sunken lounge area. At that point, the Gadowski children wanted to go with Caryn to the room, but after allowing them to accompany her to the elevator, she sent them back to their father. Dr. Raymond Gadowski, his two children, and Dr. Rosenthall would never see Caryn Campbell again.

GAGE, RUSSELL

Russell Gage was a tenant at The Oak rooming house in Tallahassee, Florida, where Bundy obtained a room in January 1978. Gage said that on the night of the attack at the Chi Omega Sorority house, he and another resident returned home around 4:00 a.m. They found Bundy staring blankly towards the university. When they spoke to him, he did not answer. Gage said Bundy joined with other residents later and offered a critique of the one responsible by saying "this was probably a professional job, and this guy has done it before."

GARFIELD COUNTY JAIL

After Bundy's daring escape from the Pitkin County Courthouse by jumping out a two and a half story window, one might be inclined to think that when Bundy was transferred to the Garfield County Jail in Glenwood Springs, Colorado, they would have made it so secure that the possibility of escape would be zero. But that was not the case. And this clownish decision would cost the lives of two women and one child in Florida, before finally, Bundy's reign of terror and murder would end.

What makes this escape so astounding is that when Bundy was placed in his cell at the jail, he noticed what everyone at the jail already knew: the light fixture in the ceiling of this one-story jail, was loose and needed welding. The story goes that they had been attempting to have it welded for a long time but it never happened. This was strange because welding something is probably something you can schedule to have done in a matter of days, even in Glenwood Springs. More likely, it just wasn't a priority. And so, with a small population of mostly non-violent prisoners in this relatively small jail, why would you place an accused murderer (on trial for the killing of Caryn Campbell), who is also suspected of being a killer of many women throughout the Pacific Northwest, in a cell that has a loose light fixture that already is of a size that a small human could fit through? Add to this Bundy's ever-present ability at scrounging up items he needed in both prisons and jails (like a hacksaw that allowed him to widen the hole just a bit), and you have a recipe for disaster. But it turns even more surreal than this: after Bundy had widened the hole to the degree that he could without making it so large that the guards would notice it and haul him out of there, he began climbing up through the hole and into the duct system so that he could learn the best way out of the Garfield County Jail. He did this on numerous nights, and the prisoners, who could hear all that racket he was making above them, promptly informed the guards as to what he was doing, which should have brought a swift response… but it didn't. The jail staff did nothing

And so, on December 30, 1977, Bundy informed the guards he wasn't feeling well, and as they passed by his cell for the rest of that night and into the next day, all they saw was a sleeping Bundy under the covers. How surprised they were when they pulled back those covers and found not the ill prisoner they were supposed to be watching, but the books and clothes he's piled them and shaped it all into a "body." Once this was finished, it was time to leave.

Bundy would make his way through the duct work, and down through a jailer's apartment who had gone out with his wife to see a movie. After changing into civilian clothes and grabbing a jacket, he was soon out into the night and Floridians, Margret Bowmen, Lisa Levy, and the young Kimberly Leach had but a short time to live.

GARZANITI, RICKEY

Rickey Garzaniti made the mistake of leaving his keys swinging in the ignition of his orange VW Bug, and Bundy was there to grab them. It was around 11:00 p.m. when Bundy spotted his favorite vehicle sitting directly across the street at 515 East Georgia Street. Unknown to Bundy, but as he was opening up the door and climbing inside, Rickey Garzaniti and his wife were inside the house picking up their child from the babysitter. Garzaniti would later tell the police that he left the keys in the car as they only expected to pick up the child and return to the VW in minutes. However, one word led to another, and it would be close to thirty minutes before the family would find an empty space where their car had been. Bundy, who had no idea how to hot wire a car in the traditional sense, must have been overjoyed to see the keys. Bundy wasted no time turning the ignition and driving away.

GAY, JERRY

Jerry Gay is a Pulitzer Prize-winning photographer who has worked for a number of newspapers throughout the years, and that includes the *Seattle Times*. It would be during his years at the *Seattle Times* that he would take a few shots one day of exhausted fire-fighters resting on a hillside, while smoke and haze drift off to their right. The picture has a surreal look to it, and resembles those you would expect to see of soldiers who had survived and were resting and gathering their wits after a particularly hard fight in a battle Perhaps this is why they would caption the pic "A Lull in the Battle." and it would be this photograph that would win

Jerry Gay the Pulitzer; and it's the only Pulitzer awarded to a photo journalist at the *Seattle Times*.

But in the world of Ted Bundy, Jerry Gay is not known for the iconic fire-fighter photo, but for the photos he took of Ted Bundy while he was housed in the Aspen, Colorado jail while awaiting trial for the murder of Caryn Campbell. Campbell, a nurse from Michigan, was kidnapped by Bundy from the Wildwood Inn in Snowmass, Colorado on January 12, 1975, and Bundy would kill Campbell within a short time after he captured her.

While Gay was with Bundy (they were shooting in the second-floor law library and in other parts of the old courthouse), he would utilize interesting angles for his photographs, and there's one shot of the killer that stands out from all the rest. To shoot this shot, Gay crawled under a large wooden table in the library and took a stunning photograph of Bundy sitting in a chair that was angled slightly off-center from the table, and as Gay snapped the shutter, he captured a picture of Bundy reading a law book with his legs crossed and shackled. And what gives it a bit of a sinister look, you can see Bundy's right eye as he's looking down at "you" with that odd gaze we've come to know from this particular killer. There are other, more normal shots of Ted Bundy which Gay took, and these are circling the Internet today. Jerry Gay spent three hours with Ted Bundy that day, and while he did not, to my knowledge, win any awards for this Bundy shoot, he has left us an excellent photographic record on that time in the life of Ted Bundy.

GELLATLY, MARVIN

Marvin Gellatly was a boyfriend of Georgann Hawkins, and was the second to last person to speak with her before she encountered Ted Bundy hobbling on crutches, wearing a leg cast, and fumbling with a briefcase. This sympathetic figure seemed very non-threatening, so when Bundy asked for help getting to his car, Georgann believed it was safe to help him. It wasn't. When contacted by the police, Gellatly answered all of their questions, but it quickly became clear that he had no information that could aid them in their search for Georgann. The last person to speak with Georgann Hawkins was Duane Covey, and you can read that story in this book.

GLENWOOD SPRINGS, COLORADO

Glenwood Springs, Colorado would play a part in the Bundy story, and there are some real ironies that enter herein. First, Glenwood Springs was where Detective Michael Fisher, who became such a thorn in Bundy's side, and who was the first investigator to have a warrant for murder placed against the killer, had his office. On March 12, 1975, Ted Bundy would purchase gas at a station in Glenwood Springs, of which Mike Fisher was familiar. This was the same day that Bundy murdered Caryn Campbell after abducting her from the Wildwood Inn just thirty miles away. When Fisher learned this, there was absolutely no doubt in his mind who was the killer of all these women: finally, Bundy's first escape from the Aspen courthouse ended in his recapture, but it would be his second escape from the Garfield County jail in Glenwood Springs that left him free to travel to Florida and murder there. Bundy's escape from his handlers at Garfield County Jail (whom the local papers referred to derisively as Keystone Cops), handlers who'd been made aware by the other inmates that Bundy had been going up through an unwelded light fixture and crawling through the duct system, and then letting himself back down into his cell, did nothing about it. And this is how Ted Bundy made his escape and went on to murder three more people (two women and a young girl) in the state of Florida.

GRAHAM, JANICE

Janice Graham, 22, was an intended Bundy victim at Lake Sammamish on July 14, 1974. She would later tell investigators that she arrived at the park around 11:30 a.m., and that while she waited for her husband and parents to arrive, she attempted to secure a picnic table but was unable to do so. She then walked over to the bandstand to watch the races. (In her testimony, Graham did not identify what type of races there were). It was here that Bundy, wearing a sling on his arm, approached Janice and said hello. She said hello back but then tried to walk away; Bundy, however, got right to the point. He asked her if she could help him unload his sailboat and she quickly agreed. But as they reached his VW and there was no sailboat or trailer to support a boat, Bundy quickly said it was just "…at my folks' house, it is just up the hill." She refused, explaining she was waiting for her husband and parents to arrive.

As they returned to the park, Bundy became apologetic for not telling her it wasn't in the parking lot. About ten minutes later, Janice Graham noticed the abduction of Janice Ott in progress. She watched Bundy walking with her as she pushed her yellow bicycle, and they were headed to the parking lot.

GRAND JUNCTION, COLORADO

Grand Junction, Colorado is forever immortalized in the Bundy murders due to the abduction and murder of Denise Oliverson on Sunday, April 6, 1975. The city is located in the western portion of the state and is but 30 or so miles from Utah. For a greater explanation of this murder, see Oliverson, Denise in this book.

Lastly, an odd twist in this case is that for many years the Denise Oliverson case has remained open, despite the fact that Ted Bundy confessed to her murder on tape, and that Detective Mike Fisher played said tape for the Grand Junction PD within days of Bundy being put to death.

GRIGGS LUMBER MILL

During the summer of 1969, Bundy worked for Griggs Lumber Mill. This was still a "low" period for Bundy, and he was struggling to put his life back together after the breakup with his girlfriend, Diane Edwards. It wasn't a breakup he wanted, and it took an emotional toll on Bundy. This spiraling downward caused him to withdraw from school in Washington State, and after heading back east to see family in Philadelphia, he enrolled at Temple University, only to leave months later and return to Seattle. Once back home he decided not to return to the university, worked menial jobs, but would see his prospects rise in September of that year when he met Liz Kloepfer who became his girlfriend for the next six years.

HAGEN, CHRIS

Chris Hagen was the name Ted Bundy starting using after he arrived in Tallahassee, Florida, and took up residence at The Oak rooming house in that city.

HAGMAIER, WILLIAM

William "Bill" Hagmaier was an FBI agent in the Behavioral Science Unit, and spent several years interviewing Ted Bundy while he was on death row. It was Hagmaier's job to get close to Bundy so that he would see the agent as a friend and perhaps open up to him. Bundy was but one murderer the BSU was interviewing, and the program, occasionally misunderstood even by other FBI agents (Bill Hagmaier told this author that he had friends within the FBI who couldn't understand why he was getting so close to Bundy), was and is a success.

HALL, DONALD M.

Donald M. Hall was an Adult Probation and Parole officer for the state of Utah, and was responsible for writing the pre-sentence investigation report for the sentencing judge, after Ted Bundy was convicted for the kidnapping of Carol DaRonch. Given Officer Hall's position, he had a good deal of interactions with Bundy, and at least on one occasion he quite accidentally pushed the wrong emotional button, and ignited a silent rage within Bundy that he was unable to conceal, causing his face to redden and become momentarily contorted. What follows is from Officer Hall's report:

It is of interest that the defendant displayed marked signs of hostility when asked about his early childhood. Specifically, when he was asked about his 'real father's whereabouts,' his face became quite contorted and reddened and he paused momentarily. He then gained composure and replied rather succinctly and [said] approximately: 'You might say that he left my mother and me and never rejoined the family.'

HAMMONS, ELZIE

Elzie Hammons, 36, was a construction worker that enjoyed hunting grouse. On the morning of September 7, 1974, he, along with his friend Elza E. Rankin, were hunting grouse, in Issaquah, and literally stumbled upon the remains of Janice Ott and Denise Naslund, both of whom were abducted by Ted Bundy on July 14, 1974 and killed that same day. A third body (without a skull) was discovered as well, and this was later determined to be the remains of Georgann Hawkins. Bundy would tell Detective Bob Keppel where he buried Georgann Hawkins' head, which, according to Bundy's directions, was close to where the other remains were found, but despite judicious searching, it was never located.

HANSON, JUDGE STEWART M.

Judge Stewart M. Hanson (1939-2008), is best known outside of Utah for his role in the Carol DaRonch kidnapping trial, where defendant Ted Bundy opted for a bench trial instead of a jury trial. His thinking was, Judge Hanson has such a good reputation for being a fair judge (which was correct), his chances of acquittal were higher through his decision alone. Judge Hanson's fairness would in fact come into play, as Bundy hoped, but after deliberating the weekend after the trial ended, found Bundy guilty of the kidnapping of Carol DaRonch. As a result, Ted Bundy received a one to fifteen-year sentence in the Utah State Prison.

HARBOR VIEW MENTAL HEALTH CENTER

In the summer of 1972, Ted Bundy went to work at Harbor View Mental Health Center. Here he would be counseling people face-to-face; unlike at the Seattle Crisis Clinic, where he was a phone counselor, and apparently did well there and had no detractors. Not so at Harbor View, where he had at least one detractor who saw Bundy as a bit of a fraud who was incapable emotionally of helping his patients and clients. Besides being a murderer, Bundy was a selfish, self-centered psychopath who had built his life around using people. So, it is somewhat odd that he chose these positions in the first place. There must have been an angle in his mind, and his decision to be working at such places must be viewed in light of what we now know about the man.

HARTER, ELIZABETH

Elizabeth Harter was a key element in the prosecution of Ted Bundy for the abduction and murder of Caryn Campbell from the Wildwood Inn in Snowmass, Colorado, on January

12, 1975. Harter had seen Bundy standing by an elevator and noticed how out of place he looked because he wasn't wearing any ski clothing or warm clothing, neither did he have any ski equipment with him. However, when Detective Mike Fisher started the long process of interviewing everyone at the Wildwood Inn (while battling the frigid sub-zero temperatures as he went from room to room), she never mentioned a "strange man" as she referred to him. However, the following year, as Fisher was re-interviewing the same guests who'd returned for their annual time at the lodge, he was told by a doctor who was a friend of Mrs. Harter, that the investigator should interview her; the doctor explaining that for the last year, she had brought up this incident on more than one occasion. This surprised Fisher, as he'd spoken to Harter the previous year but she never mentioned him. This time, however, as Fisher talked with Harter and showed her a number of photos of men, which was the equivalent of a line up, she picked out Bundy right away, and as requested by Fisher, signed and dated the back of the pictures where she'd identified Bundy. However, during the trial, when Mrs. Harter was called upon to identify the man in court, she identified an undersheriff by the name of Ben Meyers.

HAWKINS, GEORGANN

Georgann Hawkins

Georgann Hawkins (1955-1974) was a young woman attending the University of Washington during the 1973-1974 school year. Originally from Lakewood, Washington (near Tacoma), she was in her first year at the university and was doing well. She was also a sister at the Kappa Alpha Theta sorority. On the night she disappeared, her actions and movements were very routine. Because she had a Spanish test the next day, she had been studying for a part of the evening of June 10, 1974. However, during the evening she took time off to attend with a friend a frat party several blocks away.

Georgann, who'd heard the stories of the missing girls, was doing everything she knew to do to keep herself safe, including walking with someone else in the evening. It was the smart thing to do and Georgann knew it. And so, around 12:30 a.m., when she and her friend, Jennifer, left the frat party, they made their way back to the fraternity and sorority houses along Greek Row. Unbeknownst to Georgann, the one responsible for the missing women was working Greek Row – from the front of the row on 17th Avenue, to the alley behind the frat and sorority houses. So, when Georgann told Jennifer she wanted to stop and visit her boyfriend, Marvin Gellatly, in his fraternity which sits on the corner of 17th N.E. and N.E. 47th, she said she'd watch her go down the alley to make sure she was safe. But because she wasn't wearing either her glasses or contacts, she asked Jennifer to call out if everything was okay. When her friend turned around and called out that she was alright, Georgann called out she was okay too.

Georgann, who entered the frat house through the back door, spent about 30 minutes talking with Marvin before going out the same way and entering the alley. As she did so, the door slammed behind her, which caused Duane Covey to pop his head out his second-floor window to see who it was. They knew each other, so the two spent the next few minutes talking. Down the alley, shrouded by darkness, Bundy watched the brief conversation unfold. He at that time began to sense he'd be able to abduct Georgann, Georgann quickly noticed the man approaching her. Obviously injured, he was hobbling on crutches, wore a leg cast that ran from his knee to his foot, exposing his toes, and he was struggling to carry his briefcase. Certainly not a threat, she must have assumed, and as he drew near to her, he asked the young woman for help. Believing what she saw, Georgann said yes, and the two walked back up the alley, past the rear of the frat house, crossed N.E. 47th, and turned right. As they reached the corner they turned left and kept to the sidewalk, and less than a block down 17th Avenue N.E. they turned left into an unpaved parking lot void of light (only light from nearby buildings provided some illumination). Once the passenger door was opened, Georgann was doing what she was supposed to be doing, placing his briefcase in the car. Bundy, who had placed a crowbar and handcuffs behind the car, made a couple of quick movements she couldn't see, and grabbed the crowbar and knocked Georgann in the head. Quickly laying her in the car (the passenger seat no doubt removed), he turned around and grabbed the handcuffs, which had been laying on the ground next to the crowbar, and cuffed her.

From here, Bundy made his way to a spot in Issaquah. On the way there, Georgann woke up and was confused, believing he was a tutor helping her prepare for tomorrow's Spanish test. After letting her speak for a moment, Bundy again struck her with the crowbar and she was out cold. Soon after arriving at his pre-selected spot, he strangled her to death.

The Seattle, Washington alley that runs behind Greek Row where Bundy encountered Georgann Hawkins and led her away to her death on June 11, 1974

HAYWARD, SGT. BOB

Sgt, Bob Hayward (1926-2017), of the Utah Highway Patrol, has the unique distinction of arresting Ted Bundy in the early morning hours of August 16, 1975. Bundy had been hunting for a victim that evening (although he would deny it), because he not only removed the passenger seat so he could lay an unconscious woman flat in his car, but his murder kit was open and some of the contents were spilling out of the bag. He was busy smoking a joint and supposedly studying a map so he could find his way home. He was in Granger, Utah, and it was around 2:30 a.m. As the buzzed-out killer sat there, he saw headlights coming toward him go bright. Hayward, already suspicious of what he might be doing, was also aware that there had been a rash of burglaries in the neighborhood – his neighborhood – and he thought that this might be one of the culprits. Seeing the bright headlights, and immediately recognizing it was a cop, Bundy took off.

Bundy, with lights off, drove as quickly as possible for several blocks through the neighborhood, all the while Hayward right behind him with his red police lights flashing. Seeing the absurdity of it all, Bundy stopped and got out of his car. As he walked towards the officer, Hayward pulled out his .357 magnum pistol, puts it out the window and demands him to stop. Bundy was arrested for evading a police officer and hauled off to the Salt Lake County Jail. Bob Hayward was with the Utah Highway Patrol for 33 years.

HAYWARD, CAPTAIN PETE

Captain Norman D. "Pete" Hayward (1925-1993) was the head of the homicide unit of the Salt Lake County Sheriff's Office in Salt Lake City, Utah. He is also the brother of Sgt. Bob Hayward of the Utah Highway Patrol. As captain of the homicide squad, he was over the entire investigation, and the boss of lead investigator for the Bundy case, Jerry Thompson.

HEALY, LYNDA ANN

Lynda Ann Healy (1952-1974) is considered Ted Bundy's first murder victim, or at least the first after he launched himself into full time murder at the beginning of 1974. Lynda was a senior at the University of Washington, and because she was a native of Seattle, she felt right at home during her years of undergraduate work. She was preparing for her future, and she had no idea someone was coming to take it all away.

On the evening of January 31, 1974, Lynda and several friends, Joann Testa, Ginger Heath, and Pete Neil, left the rooming house at 5517 12th Street N.E. and walked the several blocks to Dante's Tavern. Here they would drink beer, have some laughs and unwind. Not suspecting anything sinister nearby, they enjoyed themselves and they left the tavern in time for Pete to get back to the house, pick up some record albums, and catch the 9:41 back to his place.

The rooming house of Lynda Ann Healy near the University of Washington. It was here, in the early morning hours of February 1, 1974, when Ted Bundy would enter through an unlocked door, and after walking down to the basement, he attacked Healy and carried her unconscious into the night. Her partial remains would later be discovered on Taylor Mountain along with other known Bundy victims.

And without their knowledge, he followed them home. After a while he would check the front door and he found it unlocked. He did not enter the home at that time. For that, he would wait until the middle of the night.

Lynda Ann Healy would be awakened by a man on top of her with his hands around her throat, choking her. He would choke her into unconsciousness. This choking produced a nosebleed, and the blood ran around her neck and got onto her nightie. Once she was unconscious, Bundy took off the nightie and hung it up in the closet. He then removed Lynda from the bed, placing her either on the floor or in a chair, and actually took the time to make the bed perfectly; so much so, that later her housemates remarked that not only was it Lynda's habit of not making her bed during the week, but when she did make it, it wasn't like that. Bundy also grabbed a backpack and some clothes.

Only the lower mandible of Lynda Healy was found at the Taylor Mountain dump site in March 1975. Indeed, Taylor Mountain, the investigators discovered, was the place where Bundy would discard the heads of his victims only. The bodies, perhaps buried on a nearby mountain, remain undiscovered.

HEATH, GINGER

Ginger Heath was a housemate of Lynda Ann Healy and was with Lynda on the last evening of her life both at Dante's Tavern and the rooming house. Also a University of Washington student, she and the other housemates would leave the rooming house shortly after their friend's abduction.

HEFFRON, LAURA

Laura Heffron was the roommate of Georgann Hawkins, and they were members of the Kappa Alpha Theta sorority, one of a number of sorority and fraternity houses along Greek Row at the University of Washington. Laura, of course, met with the detectives, as did all the women and what follows is from the investigative report based on what Laura Heffron told them:

0900 hours: Detectives to room #8 victim's room and found a Miss Laura Heffron who stated that she was the roommate of the victim. At this time numerous ladies (residents) of the frat (Author's note: the writer means sorority here) house (Kappa Alpha Theta) appeared at the room. At this time detectives requested from House Mother Mary Bates if there was an area where we could converse with the girls. We were taken to a visiting room on main floor lobby. On talking to girls whose names will appear in order of conversation, the following was obtained:

Laura Heffron: She states that she and victim were freshman at the U of W, and when she saw victim on evening prior to incident, the victim was wearing the following: navy blue good quality slacks which buttoned on the left side. These slacks were supposed to have four blue buttons but Laura stated that victim had only one button left and with this she went back to her room and obtained one Laura further stated that victim's habits were of a normal pattern. That whenever she went out, she would always let some… girl know where she was going and would always leave a telephone number. When asked if the victim was an indulgent of alcohol, she stated that she drank beer of any type, and that when she drank hard liquor it normally was Vodka mixed with a Tom Collins mix. She never seemed to get tipsy but always maintained her demeanor. Laura also stated that the victim was supposed to be going home to her parents in Tacoma on 6-13-74 (this would be upon completion of exams). Laura was then asked pertaining to any jewelry victim was wearing. She relayed that victim was wearing a rectangular shaped ring on her middle left finger. The stone was a black onyx type, with a very small diamond inserted in center of ring. The band was of gold metal. On the victim's right ring finger was a gold band ring with a small pearl inserted at the top. Victim was not wearing any wristwatch, and according to Laura, the victim's eyesight was not the best and she normally wore glasses or contact lenses. These the victim did not have with her when she disappeared. They were still in room #8 this date. Victim's teeth were good but not solid white. She had very good body stature, and the last thing recalled was that victim did have freckles about her nose. Her hair length is shorter than the photo attached to this case.

HENDERSON, PAUL

Paul Henderson (1939-2018) was an investigative reporter with *The Seattle Times* (he worked at two other newspapers prior to moving to Seattle) from 1967 through 1985. He wrote many of the articles pertaining to the missing women of 1974, as well as about Ted Bundy after his arrest in Utah in 1975. In 1982, Henderson won the Pulitzer Prize for his series of articles on a Seattle man falsely charged and convicted of rape, and his journalistic efforts led to a further investigation into the case, which ultimately turned up another suspect who then confessed to the crime. In 1985, after 23 years in journalism, he became a private investigator, and in 1988, he went to work for a non-profit organization dedicated to freeing those falsely convicted of crimes. In the years Henderson was with them, he assisted in freeing over 30 individuals who'd been wrongly convicted. One might say his was a life well-lived.

HOLLEY, SHERIFF MACK

Utah County Sheriff, Mack Holley (1922-2000) was in charge of the investigation of the murder of Laura Ann Aime. Holley was sheriff of Utah County from 1973 until 1985. However, he became a deputy sheriff with the department in 1960, making his career as a law enforcement officer span 35 years. When I interviewed retired Salt Lake County Sheriff's Office Detective, Jerry Thompson, in 2006, he told me that he and Holley talked one day, and that he did everything he could to convince "Mack" that all the cases were linked, but Holley remained skeptical. Indeed, because of statements he made years later, it appears Sheriff Holley never came on board with Ted Bundy being the killer of Laura Ann Aime.

HOMER, JOHN

John Homer and Ted Bundy first met in 1975 after Ted Bundy sought to connect himself with the Mormon Church. Indeed, Bundy would meet Larry Anderson (see this book), Carol Hall and others during this period, and not surprisingly, he was well-liked by everyone. Bundy had no trouble leading a double-life, presenting a false front, but now things were different. Detective Jerry Thompson and his people were closing in on Bundy, and when he was arrested and booked for the Carol DaRonch kidnapping, they at first did not believe it – it couldn't be Bundy, as they knew him. But after his conviction in the trial, and John Homer visited him in the Utah State Prison, he'd see and hear things from Bundy that were very unlike the man he knew. Not only did Bundy have a bad attitude, but he talked of escape. While Homer found this strange and very unlike the Ted he knew, it wouldn't be many months before additional evidence would surface that Bundy was in fact a killer of women from Utah, Colorado and Washington State. This unveiling would come as a shock to Homer and all of Bundy's Mormon friends.

HOLMES, RONALD M.

Ronald M. Holmes, an Emeritus Professor at the Department of Justice Administration at the University of Louisville, and author of numerous books on serial murder, had, for a time, a unique role and connection with Ted Bundy. During the mid-1980s, Holmes began communicating with Bundy who was being housed on death row in the state of Florida. Holmes, who had by this time interviewed a number of serial killers, got to know Bundy quite well, and apparently gained the killer's trust. In fact, when I was interviewing retired Detective, Bob Keppel, who would also gain inroads with Bundy that would lead to his own interviews with him, told me that at one time Holmes was set to become "Bundy's golden boy" and Bundy had plans to confess all his murders to him. That didn't happen, of course, as Holmes and Bundy would later have a "falling out" with each other, and their association ended abruptly.

HORN, ANDREA MICHELLE

Andrea Michelle Horn was a student at Evergreen State College, and a temporary roommate of Donna Manson in the fall of 1973. What follows is from my book, *The Bundy Murders: A Comprehensive History*, and it contains the statement Michelle gave to authorities, and why her rooming with Donna was so short-lived:

A statement taken from Andrea Michelle Horn, who was Donna's roommate from October through December 1973, said, "Donna liked to party and visit, and did so most every night until the early morning hours. She would frequently then sleep in, and not attend her classes, asking [me] to tell her what happened when I got back." Although Andrea found this irritating, it was Donna's habit of turning on the lights and stereo whenever she returned home in the wee hours of the morning which caused Andrea to seek out another place to live for the remainder of that year.

A player of the flute and a writer of poetry, Donna also had an interest in the occult and was considering a course on magic and witchcraft that was going to be offered at the University of Washington. Apparently, it wouldn't be at the university proper, but at an off-campus site nearby. When asked about this, Andrea, with perhaps a bit of sarcasm, said Donna's interest was "casual only [as] it would require too much reading for Donna, who was basically lazy."

HUGHES, PHILLIP

On October 27, 1974, Phillip Hughes and a friend were hunting in Summit County, Utah. In the early afternoon, the men came upon the body of a female, located on a brush-covered hillside. Hughes immediately called Summit County Sheriff, Ron Robinson, who, short on manpower, called the Salt Lake County Sheriff's Office. One of the responding homicide investigators, Detective Ben Forbes (partner of Jerry Thompson), described the location as follows: "The location of the crime scene is due east of the Summit Park subdivision, bordering Timberline subdivision." The body turned out to be that of Melissa Smith, abducted on October 18, 1974. And as was his habit, Bundy left the body close to where people lived and/or travelled, as if he wanted the body discovered.

IDAHO HITCHHIKER MURDER

Bundy left Washington State to attend law school in Utah around late morning or perhaps around noon of September 2, 1974. About seven hours later Bundy stopped in Nampa,

Idaho to call Liz, as they'd picnicked there once when they were traveling to see her parents in Utah. And it would be about thirty minutes after hanging up the receiver to the pay phone, and just on the outskirts of Boise, that he'd steer his VW to the emergency lane after spotting a young woman with a green backpack hitchhiking at the top of the on-ramp. She needed a ride and Ted Bundy was there to give her one.

Bundy said for the next three or four hours they traveled in an easterly direction on I-84, and because it was well after dark, and because Bundy had been eyeing a river near the highway, he turned off the highway (at the time, some of I-84 was still the older road, while other sections were newer and more efficient), and started heading for the river. At some point he picked up a crowbar from behind the front passenger seat and struck the unnamed woman in the right rear portion of her head, knocking her out cold.

At whatever spot that he stopped his VW and dragged the woman out of his car, he took her towards the river where he laid her on the ground. Again, following his usual MO, Bundy would strangle her while having sex with her from behind, either vaginal or anal. Once she was dead, Bundy probably spent some time with the corpse, as he was a necrophile, and would have been interested in having additional sex acts with her dead body. Bundy would later say that he placed her body in the river, burned her identification, and dropped the backpack in an area of Salt Lake where people were used to dumping items.

As we close out this murder it is worth noting that when I was interviewing Russ Reneau, the Idaho investigator who, along with co-investigator, Randy Everitt, listened to Bundy's final confession of the two murders he committed in the state -the Idaho hitchhiker, and Lynette Culver, 12, of Pocatello – it was suggested by Reneau that Bundy may have fabricated the story altogether. Reneau based this on their inability to locate any missing women who fit her description. Bundy had said he thought she may have been from the Boise area, but because there were no distraught families reporting missing daughters from the surrounding area of Boise, or even farther away that they could link to Bundy, nor could they obtain any leads in Wyoming where Bundy believed she was going, he felt that this information did not bolster Bundy's claims. However, this hypothesis is based completely on Reneau's opinion only, *and is not based on anything Bundy had said during his confession!*

On the contrary, Bundy answered very specific things about this young woman and he explains the narrative of that abduction, and it fits a normal pattern -indeed, Bundy said that he and the woman traveled eastward on I-84 for three or four hours. And while Bundy didn't say it, it was a departure from his usual MO of whacking his victims in the head with a hidden crowbar within a few minutes after they entered the car.

Also, Bundy was also being extremely helpful during these end-of-life confessions and was attempting to answer all of their inquiries honestly. He even said at the end of the hour-long Q&A that an hour isn't much time, and Bundy told them that if they have additional questions, he would try and answer them. And in fact, Reneau did send Randy Everitt back into the prison a little while after the scheduled meeting ended, and Bundy freely gave up additional information when asked by Everitt.

Bundy also mentioned to investigators that he couldn't remember the young woman's name and that he burned her identification. Burning the identification made perfect sense as there's always a chance someone will find it if you merely throw it away. He wouldn't leave it in the backpack, as he was taking the backpack back to Salt Lake City where he'd discard it in an area where other people were dumping items. From Bundy's perspective, destroying her ID was the correct thing to do.

In my view, all of these things point to the hitchhiker being an actual person, as Bundy said, and an actual abduction which led to her murder. In the end, I believe Ted Bundy murdered the Idaho hitchhiker just as he said he murdered her. One individual suggested that perhaps the hitchhiker story might help Bundy stay alive longer as they worked with the killer to discover information that could lead them to some solid answers. But this flies in the face of the established facts Bundy just presented: he had told them everything he knew or remembered about the murder and there would be no reason to revisit it. At this point Bundy was, without question, very tired from the marathon talks he'd been having with the investigators, his attorneys, and others. Had there been no Idaho hitchhiker murder, he would have spoken only about his other murder in the state, that of Lynette Culver.

IDAHO STATE UNIVERSITY

On May 5, 1975, Ted Bundy traveled north out of Salt Lake City for what would be a two-day hunt for a victim. His destination was Pocatello, Idaho, and Idaho State University was his target. Here, the killer believed, he'd interact with many attending females and find a suitable person to abduct. Once again, Bundy was planning and it should have gone much like he had planned it. However, the weather would foil Bundy. Even though it was officially springtime, Pocatello was still in the grip of wintry weather, and on both days the killer prowled the city and the university, cold winds and snow showers kept women moving quickly to their cars, and Bundy's attempt to stop them to talk, or act like he was injured and needed help, did not work.

It is interesting to note that it would be at Idaho State University where Bundy, for the first and last time (until his August 1975 arrest), would be confronted by an authority figure during his time of murder. It occurred while he was in the women's dormitory to search for a victim. The building was a high-rise and Bundy was on an upper floor when a male supervisor asked him what he was doing there, and asked for identification. Bundy said he didn't have any identification with him, and was told to leave the building and did so.

INTERMOUNTAIN CRIME CONFERENCE

The Intermountain Crime Conference was held in Aspen, Colorado on November 13-14, 1975. Here the investigators and others in law enforcement talked about Ted Bundy, and all present understood that Bundy was their man. He was the elusive killer of the Northwest and beyond, and now he's been revealed. It was just about putting the pieces together to bring him to judgment and everyone knew it. At the time this conference occurred, Bundy had been charged with the kidnapping of Carol DaRonch, had gone home to Seattle to see his girlfriend, Liz Kloepfer, her daughter, family and friends. He would return to Utah and stand trial in February of 1976 and ultimately found guilty.

ISSAQUAH, WASHINGTON

Issaquah, Washington will always be a part of the Bundy story for several reasons. First, there's the Issaquah "dump" site that Bundy used to discard the remains of Denise Naslund and Janice Ott (Ott's skull was never recovered), and the skeletal remains (again, minus the skull) of Georgann Hawkins. Bundy did tell Detective Bob Keppel that the Hawkins skull was buried in that location, but further searches failed to locate it. Issaquah is also where Janice Ott maintained a small apartment with a roommate. And finally, Issaquah is about five miles from Lake Sammamish State Park, and during Bundy's hunting there that Sunday, July 14, 1974, he had mentioned to a potential victim that a sailboat he needed help with was up at "his parents' house in Issaquah."

JACKSONVILLE, FLORIDA

By the time Jacksonville, Florida received a visit from Ted Bundy in February 1978, he was a far different creature than he'd been when he was abducting and murdering women in Washington State, Oregon, California, Utah, Colorado and Idaho. And so, his anticipated capture of a victim in the city would fail miserably, and part of it was no doubt the result of his lack of hygiene at this point, as well as how changed and weird his personality could be at any one moment. The closest he came to abducting a female was when he encountered Leslie Parmenter, 14, in the K-Mart parking lot. He was forced to break off the impending attack when Leslie's brother, Danny, showed up and began questioning Bundy as to what he was doing. Bundy's fear of a physical confrontation with Danny Parmenter quickly caused him to flee in the stolen FSU media van he was driving.

JONES, RANDY ALTON

Randy Alton Jones was one of two desk clerks at the Holiday Inn in Lake City, Florida, who waited on Bundy as he checked into the hotel on the evening of February 8, 1978. Jones believed Bundy was either high or drunk, said he slurred his speech, and stated his clothes were "rough."

JOPLING, JUDGE WALLACE

Judge Wallace Jopling (1917–2010) was the presiding judge over the murder trial of Kimberly Leach, who was murdered by Ted Bundy after he abducted her from Lake City Junior High on February 9, 1978. Bundy was convicted of the Leach murder, and even though he'd already been sentenced to death in the Chi Omega murders of Margaret Bowman and Lisa Levy, he would be put to death for the killing of Kimberly Leach.

KAEHLER, SHARON

Sharon Kaehler is the sister of Ted Bundy victim, Kathy Parks, and because their father had had a heart attack, she had made contact with Kathy shortly before Kathy went missing.

KATSARIS, SHERIFF KENNETH

Ken Katsaris was the sheriff of Leon County, Florida, and was charged with keeping Bundy securely housed in the Leon County Jail. He was also the head of the investigation for Leon County, and they worked closely with the Tallahassee Police Department on the Chi Omega murders. Katsaris would also prove to be a thorn in Bundy's side, and Bundy loathed him for it. When Katsaris kept Bundy in a cell with a 25 watt light bulb, refused him access to the press, and denied him exercise, Bundy filed a lawsuit against the sheriff and won.

KENT, BELVA

Belva Kent was the mother of Ted Bundy murder victim, Debra Kent. She was in fact the last person to speak with Debra only moments before she was abducted by Bundy in the parking lot of Viewmont High School in Bountiful, Utah. Bundy had no trouble capturing Debra, as she left the school before the play ended and entered a darkened and empty parking lot, Bundy caught up with her and managed to assault her before she could enter her car.

KENT, DEAN

Dean Kent (1937-2016) was the father of Debra Kent, murdered by Ted Bundy. An oil executive with Triangle Oil, Dean had been recovering from a heart attack, when, on November 8, 1974, he attended a play – *The Redhead*

– being performed at Viewmont High School where Debra was a senior. Because the play was running late and it was clear it wasn't going to let out at 10:00 p.m. as scheduled, Debra told her parents she'd pick up her brother Blair from a local roller rink as she didn't want her parents to miss the ending. That was the last time they saw their daughter.

The abduction and murder of Debra Kent effectively destroyed the emotional well-being of the Kent family, and Dean Kent was never the same. After a time, he and Belva would divorce, and their grief of losing Debra was only compounded after the death of their son, William Kent in 1984.

KENT, DEBRA

Debra Kent (1957-1974), 17, was a senior at Viewmont High School, and had been attending a play, *The Redhead*, with her parents, Dean and Belva Kent, at the school on Friday evening, November 8, 1974. She'd left the play early (it was running late) to pick up her brother Blair from a nearby roller rink. Ted Bundy, who had been pacing back and forth in the aisle that runs directly behind the last row of seats, spotted Debra as she rose from her seat and left the auditorium through the doors on the school's western side. Bundy immediately hurried out the main front doors and turned right on the sidewalk, and had to have sprinted to catch up with her. Once he did, he quickly overpowered her and placed her in his VW that was parked in the western lot as well. It is this author's opinion that Bundy did not immediately leave the school, but instead went back inside the auditorium. What follows is from my book, *The Bundy Murders: A Comprehensive History*:

Previous authors have assumed that once Bundy overpowered the unfortunate girl, he simply sped away. I believe this is incorrect, given the outward physical appearance Bundy presented just prior to Debbie Kent leaving the building, and how he looked moments later. The following is a scenario which, I believe, is far more plausible. As Debbie exited the west doors of the school's auditorium, she was wearing long white pants, a blue long-sleeved sweater with a flower in the middle, a small gold necklace, and her Viewmont High School class ring. She wouldn't have far to walk to reach the car, but it didn't matter, as Theodore Bundy was quickly closing in on her from behind. Because the play was still in progress, it is entirely possible that no one else was either in the parking lot or anywhere nearby. Whatever struggle ensued between the two (and it's likely there was at least a brief one, the duration of which may only have been seconds, but long enough for Debbie to let out a scream), Bundy quickly took control of the situation and rendered her unconscious. After knocking her out by some means, he picked up her body and transported it to his car. This left him winded, his hair askew, and part of his shirt tail hanging out. It was at this point that he re-entered the theater and was seen by the others. However, when Raelynne Shepard pointed out to her husband the odd man who'd been bothering her earlier and Bundy noticed them looking his way, he got up from his seat and left the auditorium for the last time. He didn't want a confrontation with anyone now that he had a warm body in his car.

When Bundy was finally making his end-of-life confessions just prior to his execution, he told Utah Detective Dennis Couch, that he dumped Kent's body near Fairview, Utah, and from the description the killer gave (leaving police to believe Bundy was describing Fairview Canyon), besides finding hundreds of animal bones, they also discovered the patella of a female, and the authorities believed it belonged to Debra Kent. However, the police did a strange thing: they turned the patella (evidence) over to the Kent family without determining to whom the patella might belong. However, in 2015 DNA testing was performed on the patella and it was determined that it was in fact from Debra Kent. What follows is a portion of the article from the *Deseret News* on March 12, 2019:

"At that time, this is your closure that we can give you right now," Alexander said of that gesture. He said it is unclear why police at the time gave the family that evidence, however.

Three and a half years ago, after learning the family had the patella, investigators retrieved it from the family to use for DNA testing.

"(Belva Kent) was very hesitant at first, but eventually she agreed, believing that it would be a good thing to know and have that confirmation," Alexander said. "I sent the patella to the University of North Texas as well as the samples that were collected, and then they were able to determine that the patella matched the family DNA that was collected."

The family received an official death certificate and got the patella back.

Alexander said the Kent family was grateful for the DNA confirmation.

Viewmont High School, Bountiful, Utah

WILLIAM KENT

William Kent (1958-1984), born just one calendar year after his sister, Debra, was, like the rest of the family, greatly affected by her murder. And while life went on for William (he would be married and have two children), his life would end suddenly at the age of 26 due to an alcohol-related car accident.

KEPPEL, DETECTIVE ROBERT D.

Detective Robert D. Keppel was a rookie homicide investigator when he was assigned to investigate the disappearances, and then murders, of the women of Washington State. As things got up to speed, and the Lake Sammamish abductions gave clues as to a man named Ted, Keppel became head of the "Ted Taskforce." committed to finding the killer and bringing him to justice. And yet, despite the thousands of man-hours spent trying to capture this most elusive killer, Bundy would slip out of the state on September 2, 1974 to attend law school and find a new killing ground. That said, Keppel would get to know Bundy quite well long after his capture, as he aided the Detective in Washington State's hunt for the Green River Killer. Keppel would also have his time with Bundy in his end-of-life confessions, as would all investigators who had missing and murdered women in their respective states.

KESSLER, KEN

Ken Kessler knew Ted Bundy from the time they were third-graders in Tacoma, Washington, and in fact they would go to school together through high school. It's also clear he was as aghast as anyone when it was revealed that his friend was the killer of the Northwest and beyond. What follows are his words taken from a *Tacoma News Tribune* article published on July 3, 1986:

Here is a completely normal person that has achieved success, who's well-liked and who's trusted... He's as normal as any high school kid could be. And then something happens. There would be no way of predicting that. People are now trying to go back and find strangeness, and it's just not evident. Maybe this just happens to normal people.

KILLIEN, PHIL

Phil Killien was a Seattle prosecutor, and he would have a brief, but interesting role in the case of Ted Bundy. After Ted Bundy had made bail in Utah, and was scheduled to stand trial in early 1976 for the abduction of Carol DaRonch, he decided to go home to Washington State to see his girlfriend, Liz, and family and friends, and he flew home in November 1975. Seattle authorities were determined to keep their eyes on Bundy while he was in the state so he'd think twice about killing yet another female. In fact, psychiatrists and psychologists working with the police explained to those in charge that it was important for Bundy to know they were surveilling him, and by keeping up this pressure, Bundy might not act out and commit another murder.

However, there was a small problem: Bundy's girlfriend, Liz Kloepfer, was no longer cooperating with the police (without question, she had issues with vacillating), and they were having trouble locating Bundy. Both Seattle PD and King County PD were searching for him but without success. However, on December 1, 1975, Phil Killien's sister telephoned him and said she'd spotted Bundy at the University of Washington law school, and the "chase" began.

KLEINER, KATHY

Kathy Kleiner was a Chi Omega sister who became one of Ted Bundy's living victims, after she survived the attack on her sorority house in the early morning hours of January

15, 1978. Kathy and Karen Chandler roomed together (room 8), and while they laid peacefully in their beds, Bundy was beating, strangling and murdering Margaret Bowman and Lisa Levy, both of whom were in separate rooms. And so, as Bundy turned the doorknob on room 8, he found it unlocked. What follows is from my book, *Ted Bundy's Murderous Mysteries*:

Because Kathy was not in a deep state of sleep, she said she remembered hearing the door but did not open her eyes. However, when she heard what sounded like a foot kicking the footlocker that sat between Kathy and Karen's bed (her eyeglasses were sitting on top of this footlocker as well), she opened her eyes and saw what looked like a black shadow and a club coming down at her. After Bundy struck Kathy several times with the log he'd picked up outside the sorority, Karen woke up and Bundy attacked her as well. And then, out of nowhere, it abruptly stopped when Bundy saw the car lights of what turned out to be Nita Neary's boyfriend bringing her home. Still holding on to the log (which by now had lost most of its bark), he exited the bedroom and started down the steps. Unknown to Bundy, he was spotted by Neary as he left by way of the front door.

When I was interviewing Kathy for the above-mentioned book in the spring of 2018, she explained that she'd recently undergone yet another operation on her jaw to fix something Bundy had done to her, now so very long ago.

KLOEPFER, ELIZABETH

On September 30, 1969, Ted Bundy was having a few beers at the Sandpiper Tavern, when he spotted Liz Kloepfer sitting at another table. Liking what he saw, Bundy walked over to the young woman and asked her to dance, but she declined. Bundy, perhaps a bit stung by her rejection, quickly found another woman to dance with. Soon after this, however, Liz approached him at his table, which no doubt surprised Bundy. The ensuing conversation clicked for both of them, and this began a six-year relationship that was doomed from the moment they said hello. But of course, none of this was known to Liz, and it may be that in the days ahead, Bundy himself may have considered the possibilities, however fleeting, that perhaps he could fall in love, settle down, and be normal like other people?

It's fair to say that the years Liz spent with Ted Bundy were mixed with love, happiness, sadness and doubt. And then, as the years rolled by, she found Bundy changing in ways that troubled her, including how he wanted to have sex. Suddenly, he wanted to have anal sex, desiring to tie her up, and perhaps the most bizarre of all, wanting to choke her during intercourse, the result of which on one occasion she had to "awaken" Bundy to get him to stop. None of these things were natural to Liz, and she wanted no part of them.

While all of this was going on, Washington State was being subjected to a rash of unexplained disappearances of college-aged women, and it was unlike anything the region had ever experienced. And then, on Sunday, July 14, 1974, the double abduction of Janice Ott and Denise Naslund from Lake Sammamish State Park occurred (Ott in the morning and Naslund in the afternoon). This bold abduction blew the lid off the investigation, and no longer were the previous missing women considered only disappearances- they were abductions and everyone knew it. Not only that, but they were now looking for a man named "Ted." who drove a VW Bug.

Without question, Lake Sammamish was a pivotal moment in the investigation of the missing women. But it was also a pivotal moment for Elizabeth Kloepfer. One morning a co-worker came up to Liz and showed her one of the composite drawings of the Lake Sammamish "Ted" and saying it looks like her Ted, quickly adding that her Ted also drove a Volkswagen. This began the long process whereby, at the end of this long road, Elizabeth Kloepfer would finally realize that Ted Bundy, her boyfriend of many years, and a type of step-father to her daughter, was actually the brutal and diabolical killer many investigators from many states were desperately looking for. For Liz's part, these years would be difficult, for on the one hand, she held suspicions that her Ted could be the Ted responsible for the murders. But then she'd vacillate and see the goodness in Bundy, and would then doubt her reasonings about him; a doubt that most likely produced guilt for ever having suspected him in the first place. But this vacillation could only last so long.

After Bundy escaped from Colorado for the second and last time, he made his way to Florida where he murdered Chi Omega sorority sisters, Margaret Bowman and Lisa Levy, and then his last victim, twelve-year-old Kimberly leach. He telephoned Liz after his arrest and all but admitted he was responsible for the killings at Chi Omega. And for Liz, it was the end she had suspected was coming for a very long time.

KNUTSON, LESLIE

Leslie Knutson became involved with Ted Bundy in the summer of 1975. They'd met at a party hosted by Salt Lake County prosecutor, Paul Van Dam. From all outward appearance they looked like a normal couple, and for a while they were -outwardly, for there was no denying what Ted Bundy really was. That said, Ted fully accepted her young son, Josh, and would even take Josh and a friend to the drive-in as well as a local swimming pool. He replicated the same type of husband/father role with Leslie and Josh as he had with Liz and her daughter. But there were signs of trouble that only Leslie and others close to the situation could see, and soon this relationship would, like all other relationships where Bundy was involved, die.

In 2018, I had the pleasure of interviewing Francine Bardole (see Bardole, Francine in this book), and she saw signs of disintegration in their relationship. What follows is from *Ted Bundy's Murderous Mysteries* and it gives a good picture of what Francine and her son, Larry, witnessed as things progressed:

Larry also related the story of a time when Josh asked Larry to come to his house one morning, and when he arrived, a very tired Bundy answered the door to let him in. With that, Bundy retreated back into the bedroom and shut the door. For the rest of the day, Bundy stayed in the room, and Larry noticed a food tray outside the bedroom door where Leslie had obviously brought him something to eat, and once he was finished, he simply placed the tray outside the door. Apparently, Bundy had been up all night, and then spent that day catching up on some much-needed sleep. This, of course, was nothing unusual, as Bundy the killer was a very nocturnal hunter of women. Sleeping during the day was very routine for him, and it was something that had been noticed by many others, including his girlfriend Liz.

One aspect that goes along with this has to do with the effects this sleeping pattern may have been having on Leslie and their relationship together. When I discussed this with Francine, she said the following:

There were occasions where Leslie had arranged for me to care for Josh so she could do something with Ted. It was not unusual for her to cancel at the last minute because Ted did not want to or could not go. I could hear the frustration in her voice when she called to tell me the event was off. I highly doubt Leslie did not address the issue when she did see Ted. Ted would "hole up" in the dark during the day on occasion and like Larry said, want to be left alone. I can only imagine Leslie feeling like she was walking on eggshells during these moments.

The left apartment of this duplex on Redondo Ave was the home of Leslie Knutson and her son Josh, and after Bundy started dating Leslie, he stayed here often. Courtesy Francine Bardole

KRALICEK, DEPUTY RICK

Deputy Rick Kralicek came into close proximity with Ted Bundy after Detective Mike Fisher came for Bundy at the Utah State Prison between 3:30 - 4:00 a.m., for his transfer to Colorado. It was Friday, January 28, 1977, and Bundy was being transferred to Aspen, Colorado to stand trial for the murder of Caryn Campbell, whom he abducted from the Wildwood Inn in Snowmass, Colorado. As the cuffed and shackled Bundy was led out into the cold Utah air, he was placed behind Undersheriff, Ben Myers, who was seated in the passenger seat. Sitting next to Bundy was Detective Mike Fisher, and Kralicek was the driver of the unmarked police car. Although Bundy believed the lawmen might decide to murder him during that dark, early morning drive, he was delivered unharmed to the Aspen jail later that morning.

KRAUT, DAWN

Dawn Kraut

Dawn Kraut was a senior at the University of Washington on the day she noticed Ted Bundy sitting at a lunch table in the cafeteria of the school. Bundy was not a student, but had returned to Seattle after being released from jail in Salt Lake City, and he was due to stand trial for the kidnapping of Carol DaRonch in just a couple of months. What follows is a portion of her testimony and is taken directly from Dawn's statement to police:

Date: 12-5-75

Statement of Dawn Kraut:

On Thursday, December 4, 1975, I was at the Undergraduate Library Cafeteria at the University of Washington where I am a senior majoring in Psychology and Anthropology. I had a class from 1:30 to 2:30 p.m. and then went to the cafeteria by myself. I sat alone at a table and was studying. At about 3:00 o'clock I noticed a man I recognized as Ted Bundy from the newspapers, sitting about two tables away. I had never met Bundy. I wasn't really sure it was him as I thought he was in Salt Lake City. The man I thought was Ted Bundy was talking with a hippie-type guy, he was about 25 years old and had long blond hair. Ted was eating a hamburger and laughing and smiling, although I could see under the table a kind of dichotomy – his legs and feet were moving as if he were very nervous. The blond man asked Ted what year he was in, in law school and said he had seen Ted's photograph in the paper. Ted appeared to know the blond man. I wasn't able to hear much of their conversation and when they stopped talking, the blond man and Ted got up from the table and parted. Ted was going near the door and I went toward the vending machine to get something to drink. I wasn't very far from Ted then and I quietly said, "Ted?" Ted turned around and said "Do I know you?" I said "No" and he nodded his head and asked my name. I frowned and he said, "Just your first name." I said Dawn. Ted said, "I saw you looking at me, it was more than just a double-take." I said, "I never forget a face." Then I didn't want him to think I recognized him from seeing him in person before and I told him I had seen his picture in the papers. Ted said, "The mug shots." And I said I had seen an old newsreel. Ted said he was surprised that they had kept them. At first Ted seemed nervous and then composed as we talked longer. He told me he was Ted Bundy. He was wearing nicely pressed old jeans, new reddish-brown loafers, a navy-blue turtleneck and a beige and brown striped sweater with a loose cloth belt. When he was eating his hamburger, he wasn't wearing gloves, but now he was. They were brown with leather stitching. We stood by the door and had a conversation for about 45 minutes.

In March 2019, as I was putting the finishing touches on *Ted Bundy's Murderous Mysteries*, I was contacted by Dawn Kraut, and she was both friendly and forthright about her dealings with Bundy, and passed along additional interesting background information on her strange experience with the killer, and thankfully, we had time to get it into the book.

LAKE CITY, FLORIDA

Lake City, Florida was a sleepy and quiet town back in 1978, with a population of around 10,000 people. Over the years since, it's lost some residents, only to gain them back in the years following -but not much. As of 2017, the population was just a hair over 12,000. Of course, a by-product of small towns is that (and this is just a bit of a stretch), everyone seems to know each other, and it's absolutely true that if something terrible happens in their midst, it will affect the town greatly. And such was the case when 12-year-old Kimberly Leach disappeared from Lake City Junior High on February 9, 1978, and the feeling from the start was that something terrible had happened to her. It had.

Ted Bundy had abducted the child as she was crossing the school grounds from one building to another. There was an eyewitness to her abduction, but the man believed he was watching an angry father taking his little girl home to give her a spanking. When the body of Kim Leach was discovered some two months later, and it was later revealed that it was Ted Bundy who had killed her, a minister from Lake City said the town, which had been previously known for love and forgiveness, developed a strong hatred for Bundy. And, whenever the murder of Kimberly Leach is mentioned to a local, the effects of that murder can still be seen in the townspeople's faces today.

LAKE SAMMAMISH STATE PARK

Lake Sammamish State Park, located some 15 miles east of Seattle, Washington, is a beautiful place. So beautiful, in fact, that when experienced on a bright sunny day, with lots of people around having fun, it's hard to have what one might call bad thoughts running through one's head- at least if you're normal. But on the sunny Sunday of July 14, 1974, there was an evil being traversing the large crowds of Lake Sammamish, and only diabolical thoughts were flowing through his mind. Premeditated, planned, diabolical thoughts. And that mind belonged to Theodore Robert Bundy.

By July of 1974, Ted Bundy had been murdering women on about a monthly cycle, since the first of the year. True, he'd murdered for sure in 1973, and may have sporadically killed women or young girls for many years. But Bundy had determined that Sunday, July 4th was going to be different: he would abduct two women from this popular state park on the same day. Such a thing had never been accomplished before -not in Bundy's life or the life of any other murderer. And what would make the murders of Lake Sammamish so incredibly different, is that Bundy would be exposing himself to thousands of people (there were some 40,000 in attendance that day), as he led these women to their deaths. And to top off his extreme arrogance, he'd be using his actual first name.

The first to fall to his wiles was Janice Ann Ott, a probation and parole officer who once had lived in Seattle but was now living in Issaquah, Washington, only five miles from Lake Sammamish. Bundy had been attempting to lead other women away but was unsuccessful in doing so. He was playing an injured man, and he had one of his arms in a sling. Bundy would return to the park in the afternoon. He wasn't satisfied with the taking of one victim. He wanted a second one too.

At around 4:20 p.m., Denise Naslund awakened from a nap brought on by the downers and beer she's consumed earlier in the day. In fact, the three people in her party were asleep as well, so Denise didn't bother waking anyone as she knew she'd be back in a matter of minutes. Except for the presence of Ted Bundy, she would have. Slowly rising to her feet, Denise began the short walk to the restroom at the far end of the park (now torn down), and made it inside the restroom without being stopped.

In the fifteen minutes prior to Bundy encountering Denise Naslund, he had stopped and spoken with at least three women, but all turned him down and would not help him with his "sailboat" ruse. By 4:30, Bundy was standing near the entrance to the bathroom, and as Denise came out, he stopped her. Whatever ruse he used, it worked, and Denise left with Bundy and never returned.

The double abductions/murders from Lake Sammamish State Park that July 14, 1974, was a pivotal moment in several ways: first, the park itself will forever be known for the terrible thing Bundy pulled off that day. It was also a pivotal moment for all Washingtonians, as no longer would these strange disappearances be considered strange disappearances. They were now abductions, and everyone now expected this to end badly for the missing ones. But Lake Sammamish was also pivotal for Ted Bundy as well. He left clues to his identity here: they would now be looking for a man named "Ted" who drove a beige or light brown VW Bug. The testimonies of the women who'd interacted with Bundy, but who refused to go with him, helped police sketch artists create composite drawings of the man. And it would be a co-worker of Liz Kloepfer, that after he showed her a composite and teased her that it looked like her boyfriend, Ted Bundy, and that he drove a VW too, that caused Liz to wonder whether it could be true – and coupled with some of the strange things Ted had done, soon culminated in a call to the authorities. And finally, it was a pivotal last day for Denise Naslund and Janice Ott.

The skeletal remains (partial remains, actually), of Janice Ott and Denise Naslund were discovered on September 7, 1974, not far from a logging road at what has come to be known as the Issaquah dump site. They were discovered by two grouse hunters who immediately contacted the police. A third victim (Georgann Hawkins) was located as well, but her identity would remain unknown for some time. Bundy would later tell Washington Detective Bob Keppel, during his end-of-life confessions, that he had severed her head and buried it on a hillside not too far from where he'd placed the bodies. A search of the crime scene in 1989 did not locate her skull. The skull of Janice Ott has never been recovered either.

LARAMIE, WYOMING

Laramie, Wyoming is one of the stops where Bundy purchased gas as he travelled to Colorado to hunt for victims. Because Bundy was a creature of habit, it's possible, and perhaps likely, he stopped in Laramie on more than one occasion, and if so, may have used the same service station to fill up his car.

LARSEN, RICHARD W.

Richard W. Larsen (1928–2001) had a career in journalism spanning 50 years, and 23 of those were with the *Seattle Times*. In his time there he rose to associate editor, and while he wrote about various subjects and numerous people, his real passion was writing about politics. And it would be in this political arena that he would meet and interview Ted Bundy. However, once Bundy was charged with the kidnapping of Carol DaRonch and his uncovering was finally occurring, Larsen made contact with Bundy and, despite his love for political writing, he made Bundy his object of investigation and from this came his bestselling book, *The Deliberate Stranger*, which was also made into a made-for-TV movie. Larsen had a cameo role int the show as well. Richard Larsen died after a long struggle with cancer.

LEACH, KIMBERLY DIANNE

Kimberly Dianne Leach (1965-1978) of Lake City, Florida, was Ted Bundy's last victim. On the morning of February 9, 1978, as 12-year-old Kimberly Leach was crossing the school grounds between two buildings, she was spotted by Bundy who immediately stopped the stolen white FSU media van in the middle of US 90, the highway running in front of the school (blocking traffic). Bundy, who'd been seeking a victim the previous day without any success, very much wanted to grab a child from Lake City Junior High, as soon as he came upon it and considered the possibilities, he kept circling the property. There were times when Bundy had this uncanny sense that he was about to obtain a victim, and this may have been one of those times, prompting him to keep circling the property.

Getting out of the van, Bundy quickly made his way over to the child and took control of her, placed her in the passenger side of the van and sped away. A fireman, Andy Anderson, who'd just completed his shift, was on his way home when he noticed what looked to him like and angry father taking his child home.

Having escaped the scene unhindered and not being pursued, Bundy would drive some 40 miles to the Suwannee National Park, and here, in an isolated area, he would slice the throat of the young girl while he was having sex with her from behind; leaving her body underneath a low to the ground, tin hog shed. Kimberly's body would not be discovered by authorities for two months. Even so, given where he'd placed her, it's surprising she was found at all. Although Bundy had committed many murders by this time, and while he would be convicted and sentenced to death for the two Chi Omega murders, it would be the murder of Kimberly Dianne Leach that would put him in the electric chair on January 24, 1989.

LEE, OFFICER DAVID

Officer David Lee, of the Pensacola Police Department, was on his usual patrol at approximately 1:30 a.m., February 15, 1978, when he spotted an orange VW sitting behind a closed restaurant. A quick check of the plate number told Lee the car had been stolen. Bundy, who saw what was happening, put the VW into gear and tried to make a run for it but in reality, he understood he couldn't outrun the police. Bundy stopped the vehicle and waited for the cop to make his next move. When he did so, he ordered Bundy to lay on his stomach and he did so. But as Officer Lee was attempting to handcuff his suspect, Bundy rolled over and punched the officer in the face before kicking his legs out from under him. Bundy then lunged at him and Lee fired one shot at Bundy but missed. As Bundy fled (with one handcuff on his wrist, and one dangling), Lee chased him through the streets of Pensacola. More than once Bundy turned to see how close Lee was, and because the dangling handcuff kept reflecting light, Lee believed he might have a pistol. Taking careful aim, Lee fired once more, and Bundy fell to the ground. This time Lee believed he'd hit him. However, as Lee bent over to see where he'd hit Bundy, the unwounded killer once again kicked Lee's legs out from under him. But instead of fleeing, Bundy attempted to disarm him. And Lee responded by hitting Bundy three times in the face with the heavy barrel of his service revolver. Stunned and injured, Bundy surrendered, and the most dangerous man in the United States was once again in custody.

LEGAL MESSENGERS, INC.

Legal Messengers, Inc., was located at 216 James Street in downtown Seattle. Ted Bundy worked there from September 1969 until May of 1970. It should be noted there are two reports about the cause for Bundy's termination with the company. The first is that Bundy was laid off when the company merged with another company, and with no seniority, they cut him. The other story is that he failed to show up to work one day and was fired. Perhaps they're both true and that both factored into their decision to let him go.

LEIDNER, CHARLES

Charles Leidner was Bundy's court-appointed attorney to defend him in his trial for the murder of Caryn Campbell. The pre-trial hearings began in April 1977, and upon completion of these hearings, Bundy's petition to Judge George Lohr, that he be allowed to act as co-council, was granted. Bundy, who loved to maintain control over his own fate – often to his own hurt as would be seen later during the Florida trials - felt this was the best decision. Part of the reason Bundy wanted to be partly in the driver's seat of his defense, was his lack of confidence in Charles Leidner. Of course, there was absolutely no reason to feel this way as Leidner was fully competent to wage this legal battle to save Bundy's hide, but in Bundy's mind, no one could compare with the representation he received at the hands of his Utah attorney, John O'Connell. Apparently, Ted Bundy was O'Connell's biggest fan.

In the end, however, it wouldn't matter who was representing Bundy, for on June 7th of that year, Bundy escaped by jumping 25 feet to ground from the second story window in the Aspen courthouse. After his capture almost a week later, Leidner and any other counsel that were participating, were barred from representing Bundy any further as they were now witnesses to a crime (his escape), and would be called to testify against him.

LEVY, LISA

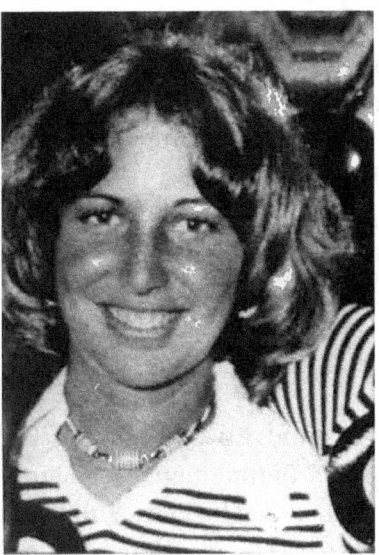

Lisa Levy

Lisa Levy (1957-1978) was a Chi Omega sister that was murdered by Ted Bundy in the early morning hours of January 15, 1978. Lisa had been sleeping alone in room 4 when Bundy attacked her. Although she was severely beaten, her death was due to strangulation. Bundy, in a fit of animalistic rage, twice bit the buttocks of Lisa Levy (and almost in the same place), and it would be this that proved to be indisputable evidence that Theodore Robert Bundy was her killer.

LEWIS, DR. DOROTHY OTNOW

Dr. Dorothy Otnow Lewis is an American psychiatrist who has had a career working with violent offenders, and in particular murderers, including Ted Bundy. In her book, *Guilty By Reason Of Insanity: A Psychiatrist Explores The Minds Of Killers*, said the following about working with Ted Bundy: "It was my job to determine whether any psychiatric problems had been overlooked that were relevant to his case. This was my job -no more, no less. He, in turn, permitted me to study him on the chance or in the hope that I would discover the forces within him and around him that had made him so extraordinarily violent." This coincided with Bundy's own wishes, as he had once expressed a desire to Det. Bob Keppel to know why he ended up committing murder; something Keppel and all cops do not see as their first matter of concern.

LINDVALL, DETECTIVE MATT

Detective Matt Lindvall of the Vail, Colorado PD was assigned the Julie Cunningham case, and Lindvall had a personal connection in that he knew Julie. Of course, the Julie Cunningham case was one of disappearance but not murder; or at least not yet. When Ted Bundy decided to come clean, and he telephoned Colorado Detective Mike Fisher telling the detective he wanted to confess to the murders, and where they discussed certain aspects of the case over the phone, a meeting was set up. Because Fisher had been investigating all of the cases in Colorado, including Cunningham's (not to mention his investigations into the murders in Utah as well in his hunt for 'similar transactions'), the detectives would do the interview of Bundy together. Their time with Bundy came on January 23, 1989, only one day before Bundy's execution.

LITTLE, KENNETH

Kenneth Little was the boyfriend of Denise Naslund (they had been living together for the past nine months), and neither he nor Denise had any plans to go to Lake Sammamish that Sunday, July 14, 1974. That pivotal decision came when the phone rang that morning. It was their friends, Bob Sargent and Nancy Battema, asking them if they wanted to go to the park that day. Although they had been very busy that weekend, and Bob later told authorities he was tired, they decided to go. As was the custom of young people in the 1970s, drugs, marijuana, and alcohol would be a part of their day, as Bob Sargent would later tell investigators: *"en route to the park, Denise, Ken, and myself each ate four valiums."*

LOHR, JUDGE GEORGE

Judge George Lohr had, one might say, two roles in the Ted Bundy murders. First, when he was presented convincing evidence by Investigator Michael Fisher, that Ted Bundy had in fact, killed Caryn Campbell on March 12, 1975, after he abducted her from the Wildwood Inn in Snowmass, Colorado, he signed the first warrant for murder against Bundy. And second, he would oversee the trial from the old courthouse in Aspen, Colorado. Judge Lohr would also grant Bundy's petition to act as co-counsel in the trial, and in fact, would show Bundy the same impartiality that he would with any attorney; and in fact, would often side with Bundy whenever he filed a brief with the judge requesting intervention in particular matters.

LUBECK, BRUCE C.

Bruce C. Lubeck was a part of Ted Bundy's Utah defense team, headed by John O'Connell, during his trial for the abduction of carol DaRonch.

MACKIE, CAPTAIN NICK

Captain Nick Mackie, of the King County Police, is a prominent face and name in the investigation of the Ted Bundy murders in that state. Captain Mackie, like all the investigators under him, was in the unenviable position of finding an elusive killer of women who had started killing in the middle of the night, and by July 1974, had advanced to abducting women in broad daylight; and not just one woman but two at Lake Sammamish on the 14th of that month.

One of the most telling statements from Captain Mackie is one that struck the public like a lightning bolt, and it confirmed the fears of many who suspected, but didn't want to believe it to be true. On September 7, 1974, the partial skeletal remains of three victims were discovered at what has come to be known as the Issaquah dump site. Those discovered were Janice Ott (minus her skull), Denise Naslund, and a third victim that authorities could not identify until Bundy, during his end-of-life confessions, told Detective Bob Keppel, that the third victim was Georgann Hawkins (Bundy said he buried the skull of Hawkins on a hillside away from where the rest of the remains were placed, but a search never located it).

When Mackie made the public announcement of the macabre find, and what it meant for the community, he succinctly and accurately said: "The worst we feared is true."

MANSON, DONNA GAIL

Donna Gail Manson (1954-1974) was a student at Evergreen State College in March of 1974, when she had the misfortune of encountering Ted Bundy. In many ways, the layout of the college was a predator's dream: constructed in the midst of a thick forest of fir trees, the designers created a place that, in a perfect world, would be one of the nicest schools to attend, as they blended the natural world with what humanity had to offer. In this setting it is very easy to feel that nature has almost completely engulfed you. And if this world was a peaceful Utopia it would all work out so well. But in the case of Donna Manson, the trails that run through the campus, always shrouded in trees, became the perfect place for a serial killer to hunt women.

On a slightly rainy March 12, 1974, around 7:00 p.m., Donna Manson headed out into the night, and took a trail, shrouded in trees, that would take her to the outside of the side of the library, and she would have made the short walk around the front corner of the building and enter the front doors. There was a jazz concert being offered and Donna did not want to miss it. However, no one remembers seeing Donna either on the trail, or enter the patio area on the building's side, or inside the library itself. Whatever happened to Donna Manson likely happened very quickly and occurred on the trail.

Either by ruse or by force, Bundy captured her and led her away to her death. Bundy would later tell that this night was akin to a blur because of the alcohol consumption, and it also appeared he didn't want to talk about it. When asked about her murder by Detective Bob Keppel, Bundy said he burned up Manson's skull in Liz Kloepfer's fireplace; a feat that may be impossible to accomplish. He also mentioned he discarded the rest of her remains in the Cascade Mountains.

One of the many secluded trails at Evergreen State College in Olympia, Washington where Donna Manson disappeared on March 12, 1974.

The library at Evergreen State College, to where Donna Manson was heading when she disappeared from a secluded walkway on the campus on March 12, 1974.

MATTHEWS, GARY

Gary Matthews was an EMT who, along with his partner, Charles Norvell, made the run to Chi Omega shortly after Bundy attacked the sorority in Tallahassee, killing two and seriously injuring two. Having arrived at one scene of carnage, they didn't realize that in short order they'd be heading off to another shocking assault on an FSU female. What follows is from *The Trail of Ted Bundy: Digging Up the Untold Stories*:

EMTs Gary Mathews and Charles Norvell arrived in the ambulance called to the Chi Omega house. Met by a sea of cops and distraught coeds, they were quickly ushered upstairs. As they reached the top of the steps, Mathews broke off from Norvell and entered one of the bedrooms, where he found Kathy Kleiner and Karen Chandler.

The light was on, and he saw immediately that both women were bloody and in a daze. There was blood on their faces, heads and on the bed. What Gary Mathews couldn't see as he worked on the women and prepared them for transport to the hospital, were three of Kleiner's teeth that were left on the bed. Both women also had broken jaws.

The night of mayhem was not over yet for Mathews and Norvell. After making the run to Chi Omega and the hospital, they drove with lights and siren blaring to an apartment at 431-A Dunwoody, the duplex home of Cheryl Thomas. The home, only four blocks from the Chi Omega house, was Bundy's second attack site of the evening.

Thankfully, Bundy was not able to kill Thomas, after the intervention of her neighbor in the duplex, Debbie Ciccarelli. Ciccarelli heard strange noises coming from next door (Cheryl crying and someone walking around) and kept calling out to Thomas through the wall, calling her phone and pounding on the wall. Bundy, who had beaten Cheryl about the head with the log, and was planning to rape and kill her, changed his mind because of all the commotion coming from next door, and quickly relieved himself instead through masturbation. Bundy then left through the same window he'd entered.

As Mathews and his partner entered Cheryl Thomas' apartment, they could see how badly she'd been beaten. What they couldn't see was that, like Karen Chandler and Kathy Kleiner, Thomas' jaw was also broken. The same log that Bundy had kept with him after he left Chi Omega, and which he used to attack Thomas, was found lying on the bedroom floor.

MCBRIDE, DR. STANLEY

Dr. Stanley McBride of Dearborn, Michigan, was the dentist of Caryn Campbell, and was called upon by Colorado detective, Mike Fisher, to provide copies of her dental records so that they could make what they believed would be a positive ID of the body found along Owl Creek Road. On February 18, 1975, the records confirmed that the body was that of "Caryn Eileen Campbell."

MCCHESNEY, KATHY

Kathy McChesney was a young investigator working alongside Detective Robert (Bob) Keppel, Keppel's partner, Detective Roger Dunn, and others within the King County Police. They became known as the Ted Taskforce, and the team would work tirelessly to catch the elusive killer that had been leading women to their deaths throughout the state. McChesney would go on to a 24-year career with the FBI, and would end her time with the Bureau as Executive Director, the third highest position in the FBI.

MCCLURE, RALPH

Ralph McClure was County Commissioner, in Salt Lake City, Utah, and unlike Ted Bundy, was a Democrat. Even so, in January 1975, Bundy applied for the job of administrative assistant to McClure, and McClure, who liked Bundy's political resume, almost hired him.

MCKIBBEN, DAVID ALLISON

In 1974, David Allison McKibben was the owner of the Suds Shop Laundromat in Issaquah, Washington. On Sunday morning, July 14, 1974, while cleaning up around the place, Janice Ott, who lived across the street, came in to do her laundry for the week. The two struck up a conversation, and as McKibben was getting close to finishing his work, he asked Janice if she wanted to walk down to Fasona's restaurant to get a cup of coffee, and she accepted. First, however, they walked back to her place so she could drop off her laundry. When she came out, they headed to Fasona's and sat for a while, drinking coffee and learning about each other.

McKibben would later give the police a detailed report of their conversation, and once they were finished, he walked her back to her apartment and the two said goodbye. David McKibben then drove to his home in North Bend, Washington, and Janice Ott went back into her apartment and changed her clothes. Soon after this she taped a note to her door stating she was going to Lake Sammamish for the afternoon. After this, she grabbed her yellow 10-speed bicycle and peddled the five miles to the park.

MCMILLAN ELEMENTARY SCHOOL

McMillan Elementary School, located at 315 East 5900 South, in Murray, Utah, is where it all began to go wrong for Ted Bundy in the early evening of November 8, 1974, for this is where he attacked Carol DaRonch after abducting her from The Fashion Place Mall. For the full story, see DaRonch, Carol in this book

MCPHEE, CHRISTY

Christy McPhee was the boyfriend of Kathy Parks, a victim of Ted Bundy who was abducted from Oregon State University on May 6, 1974, transported back to Seattle, and killed soon thereafter. It's clear Christy and Kathy were in love; or perhaps, it might be better to say that at one time they were equally in love, because the relationship changed over time. Christy's commitment toward Kathy had increased, which is perfectly natural with people in love, and he was thinking about marriage and a life-time commitment. Kathy, however, had recently made it clear, that while she did in fact love him, she was nowhere near wanting to settle down. As can be expected, this did not sit well with McPhee. Still, she hadn't broken up with him, and Christy wasn't willing to give up on the one he loved. And but for the presence of Ted Bundy on the Oregon State University campus around 11:00 p.m. on May 6, 1974, things may have worked out between them. Indeed, Christy was going to leave his home in Berwick, Louisiana to visit her, and on the night she disappeared, she mailed a letter to him in which she expressed her love for him. What follows is from her last letter: *Well - I'm looking forward to seeing you - very much. When you come, please put your arms around me and make me feel everything's OK. I'm needing the comfort of your presence now. I love you, Kathy.*

MENTZER, DR. RICHARD H.

Dr. Richard Mentzer was responsible for comparing the dental charts of Caryn Campbell, that had been received from Caryn's dentist in Michigan, in the hope that the body that was discovered days earlier on Owl Creek Road would prove to be hers. After comparing the charts of the deceased and that of Caryn's, Dr. Mentzer told the authorities that in his "unqualified opinion ... after comparing the dental charts and x-rays with the dental work on the body, that the body is in fact Caryn Eileen Campbell."

MERRILL, DAVID

David Merrill is an American journalist and co-author of the book, *Ted Bundy: The Killer Next Door.*

MESSIER, FRANCIS

Francis Messier was a young woman that lived in the same rooming house as Ted Bundy, at 409 College Avenue in Tallahassee, Florida. Messier, who caught Bundy's eye – not for murder, but for someone to date – would be the recipient of Bundy's friendly advances, and for a couple of weeks they hit it off well and had no problems. Indeed, the day after he raped and murdered young Kimberly Leach from Lake City, Florida, Bundy took Francis Messier to Chez Pierre, a popular and posh French restaurant in Tallahassee. Or, to be more exact, it was a stolen credit card that allowed them to dine there the evening of February 10, 1978. Bundy loved the place so much, that he returned the next night and had a second meal on the stolen credit card. Later, when interviewed by the police, TV reporters and the print media, said she never saw anything strange out of Bundy.

MEYERS, UNDERSHERIFF BEN

Undersheriff Ben Meyers came into close proximity with Ted Bundy when he, Detective Mike Fisher, and Deputy Rick Kralicek, escorted Ted Bundy from the Utah State Prison where he was currently housed for the abduction of Carol DaRonch, so that he could stand trial in Aspen, Colorado for the killing of the visiting Michigan nurse, Caryn Campbell. Meyers was no doubt around Bundy often, the drive the lawmen took with the cuffed and shackled Bundy would be an interesting one indeed, and you can read about it in *The Bundy Murders: A Comprehensive History.*

MIAMI, FLORIDA

Although the Chi Omega murders occurred in Tallahassee, the trial was moved to Miami, Florida as Bundy's legal team did not believe he could obtain a fair trial in Tallahassee. That trial, which began on July 23, 1979, would culminate in a guilty verdict for Bundy, and subsequently, a sentence of death in Florida's electric chair.

MICHAUD, STEPHEN G.

Stephen Michaud is the co-author, along with Hugh Aynesworth, of *The Only Living Witness: The True Story of Serial Sex Killer Ted Bundy* and *Ted Bundy: Conversations with a Killer*. Having worked for Newsweek for several years, where he wrote articles on a range of topics, including the infamous Texas 'Candy Man' murders of 30 young men and boys, he moved on to Business Week in 1977. And it was while here that he received a call from his agent that would place him in direct contact with the incarcerated Ted Bundy. Apparently, Bundy believed an independent investigation would help clear his name, and Michaud, at least considering the possibilities of what an investigation might uncover, agreed to take on the project. Michaud and Hugh Aynesworth teamed up together, and while Michaud began the long road of interviewing the accused killer, Aynesworth traveled west to investigate the murders Utah, Colorado and Washington State. Despite Bundy's hopes, their investigation would not exonerate him. But it would give the world an up close and personal look into the mind of this very unique serial killer.

MILLER, OFFICER MITCH

Tallahassee Police officers, Mitch Miller and Gerald Payne, were the first to arrive at Cheryl Thomas's duplex at 431-A Dunwoody Street, after her friend and neighbor at 431-B, Debbie Ciccarelli had called police to alert them that something was wrong with her friend. Ciccarelli had been concerned because she believed she'd heard someone crying and "pleading with someone." as well as pounding noises that was followed by silence. Because she could not get Cheryl to answer her phone, and because there was no response as Debbie called out to her through the thin wall separating the two apartments, she made the call to authorities. For the complete story, see: Thomas, Cheryl in this book.

MILLER, RALPH

Ralph Miller was the fictitious name (but based on one of the stolen credit cards) Bundy used when he checked into the Holiday Inn in Lake City, Florida on February 8, 1978. While there, Bundy, who was clearly in decline, continued to use the name Miller as he signed his bar and dinner bills, but introduced himself to the bartender as Mr. Evens.

MINERVA, MICHAEL

Michael Minerva was lead public defender for Ted Bundy in Florida prior to the two trials that would culminate in convictions and death sentences for Bundy. At the start of their association, Minerva firmly believed that the only way to save Bundy's life was to convince him to plead insanity. Otherwise, he rightly understood, Florida was going to kill him; a sentiment also shared by an attorney Bundy greatly respected, Millard Farmer out of Atlanta, Georgia (due to a legal technicality, Farmer could not practice in Florida, but he was often there advising Bundy, along with Minerva, on what he should do). But Bundy, far too arrogant to ever admit to "insanity" even if it would save his life, rejected the idea completely. And so, gift number one to save his life was cast away. Gift number two, when it arrived, would also be rejected by Bundy, and with much fanfare. Michael Minerva had secured a deal for Bundy with Larry Simpson, the chief prosecutor for the Chi Omega murders. Without question, it was a sweet deal Bundy was offered: if he would come into court and admit to the murders of Lisa Levy, Margaret Bowman, and Kimberly Leach, he could live out his life in a Florida prison, with no possibility of parole. After much cajoling from Minerva and many others as well, Bundy half-heartedly agreed to the deal and even signed a document to the court stating his intentions. However, on the morning he was to present his confession in open court, Bundy, having been warned to offer the confession without making any additional statements, immediately fired his attorneys and then ranted for a few minutes about his former counselors. Having gotten this off his chest, Minerva would later explain, Bundy then wanted to make his confession, but the prosecutors, who had patiently listened to Bundy's diatribe, told his defense team the deal was off.

MISNER, KENNETH RAYMOND

Kenneth Raymond Misner was a former student and well-known trackstar at Florida State University. He was also the victim of identity theft at the hands of Theodore Robert Bundy, who'd heard of the man and decided to obtain a copy of his birth certificate, and did so. And after Bundy's arrest in Pensacola, Florida, after struggling with patrol officer, David Lee, he identified himself as Kenneth Raymond Misner. For a while the detectives grilling him had no reason to doubt it. However, after receiving a phone call from the real Kenneth Misner, the investigators know they were back to square one as to the true identity of who was seated before them.

MOON, OFFICER KEITH L.

Officer Keith L. Moon, with the Issaquah Police Department, had an interesting, if not humorous run on October 19, 1974. Its inclusion here is due to its connection to the Bundy case, even if it was only a prank. That said, we don't know who committed the prank, so even with this, there's a sense of mystery about it. What follows is from the Issaquah PD:

Issaquah, Washington
Police Department

On approximately October 19, 1974, at approximately 0200 hours, this officer was advised by a citizen of a possible body in the roadway on I-90 at the train trestle. This officer went up with the citizen and observed a dummy in the eastbound lane of I-90. This was approximately the third dummy this officer has seen below the trestle. I took the dummy and threw it in the woods by the trestle. Two days later this officer went back and looked at the dummy close-up and saw that it had a white sweatshirt with a caricature of two pigs "humping." One was labeled Smith and the other Mott. This was on the front of the shirt. Also on the front in black felt pen was the wording "Ted Lives." On the sleeve it appeared to read "Ted + IPD + Smith + Mott." This was difficult to read though. The sweatshirt was white and appeared to be small or medium size. I took the sweatshirt back to the station as I thought Mott or Smith might be interested in the caricature of the pig. I showed this to Sergeant Mott and Paula Ralph. I then disposed of the sweatshirt. There was also a pair of pants left at the trestle. They were tan-brown corduroy of medium size and good condition... The handwriting appeared to be juvenal (sic). This officer checked on the pants on November 8, 1974. They had been removed from underneath the trestle.

MOORE, JACQUELINE

On the morning of February 9, 1978, Jacqueline Moore, the wife of a Lake City doctor, was driving east on U.S. 90 (not an expressway, but a four-lane highway), in Lake City, Florida, when she saw a white van driven by Ted Bundy coming towards her driving erratically, and according to her testimony, the van nearly "ran her off the road." As she passed the van, she saw the driver was looking down and that his head was "bobbing." Also mentioned that his mouth was open and his jaw was slack. What she didn't know was that the driver was struggling with a child – Kimberly Leach, 12, whom Bundy had abducted minutes before from Lake City Junior High.

Bundy, oddly having his mouth open and his jaw being slack, is indicative of the altered state killers can enter once they have their prey in hand, and the stages of murder are already in process. Indeed, it can be considered almost a type of trance-like state, and it will not dissolve until the murder, and all the activities of murder, are complete. Then Bundy would return to what he would refer to as his normal self. Kimberly Dianne Leach would die before an hour was out and it would be some two months before authorities would recover her remains.

MORRIS, FRANK

On November 11, 1975, Detective Roger Dunn (Detective Bob Keppel's partner), of the King County Police, interviewed a Frank Morris concerning his interactions with Ted Bundy, and what Morris tells the Detective is more accurate than even Morris may realize. What follows is taken directly from Detective Dunn's report:

1500 hrs. Frank Morris called the office to say he first met Bundy during the '72 elections when Bundy was working on the Evans campaign and he was working on the Lud Kramer campaign. He thought (Bundy) was a handsome guy who would have no trouble getting dates with girls and never noticed anything out of the ordinary. Morris succeeded Bundy as Davis' assistant when he left to go to law school and that was the last time he saw him. Morris offered an explanation that I had never heard concerning Bundy. He kept referring to all of the cases as "sex crimes" and that if Bundy were involved it would be because Bundy could not get off through straight sex and had to get into perversions to get satisfied.

MOTT, SGT. EDWARD O.

Sgt. Edward O. Mott, badge # 132, with the Issaquah Police Department, shares an interesting place in the Bundy case, and for more than being one of the officers to participate in the investigation of the disappearance of Janice Ott and Denise Naslund from Lake Sammamish State Park on July 14, 1974. Strangely, Sgt. Mott's name (along with the names of others) became what is most likely just a prank, and I must say, I would have wished this piece would have been kept as some type of "evidence." For the full story, see Moon, Officer Keith L.

MOTTRAM, ROBERT H.

Robert H. Mottram was a columnist and editor for the *Tacoma News Tribune* from 1973 – 2000, and covered mostly true crime and politics, and as such, authored a number of articles about the plight of the missing women of Washington State, and then after his arrest, Ted Bundy. Mottram previously worked for the Associated Press from 1966 – 1973, and is the author of several books.

MURRAY, UTAH

Murray, Utah will forever be connected to the Ted Bundy story because it is where Carol DaRonch had an encounter with Ted Bundy at the Fashion Place Mall that led to her abduction and almost murder. For the full story, see DaRonch, Carol in this book.

NAMPA, IDAHO

Liz Kloepfer (writing as Liz Kendall), in her book, *The Phantom Prince*, recounts how Bundy, while driving to Salt Lake City to attend law school, stopped in Nampa, Idaho, and telephoned her. This is also where they'd stopped and had a picnic on one of their drives home to see her parents in Utah in previous years. Without question, it was a nostalgic moment for the couple. Soon after their loving conversation ended, Bundy would pick up a hitchhiker on the outskirts of Boise, Idaho, just twenty miles east of Nampa on I-84. For the full story of the killing of the Idaho hitchhiker, see Idaho hitchhiker murder in this book.

NASLUND, DENISE

Denise Naslund

Denise Naslund (1955-1974), was one of two victims abducted by Ted Bundy at Lake Sammamish State Park on July 14, 1974. Denise disappeared in the late afternoon, around 4:30 p.m. after Ted Bundy had stopped her as she was coming out of the restroom, and by a ruse, he convinced her to leave the park with him, and she no doubt believed she'd be back shortly. Soon after this, Bundy took control of her, and he transported her to an unknown location, probably in the woods of Issaquah, and when they reached the destination, Denise Naslund saw Janice Ott. Ott, whom

Bundy had abducted (again by ruse) that morning from the park, had to bear the brunt of repeated sexual assaults by Bundy, prior to him securing her, possibly to a tree with her mouth most likely gagged. Because Bundy had expended most of his sexual energy on Ott, he may have had but one sexual encounter with Naslund before he killed one woman in front of the other; or so he confessed to Bill Hagmaier, the FBI agent with whom he'd become "friends" over the last several years of Bundy's life.

The death of Denise Naslund destroyed the emotional life of her mother, Eleanore Rose. And to make matters not just worse, but far worse, is that King County authorities maintained that they needed to keep the remains – bones – of Denise for evidence which is exceedingly strange and absurd, as once the investigation into each murder throughout the country is completed, the bodies are always turned over to the family. So, in this case, they "loaned" Denise's remains to the Naslund family for a funeral and mass, and then were returned to the safe care provided them by King County. However, several years later, it was discovered that King County had lost, not just the bones of Denise, but the remains of two additional Bundy victims as well. It was Washington State tax dollars hard at work.

Speaking of tax dollars, two of the families that suffered the needless indignity of having their loved ones' remains forever taken from them, filed a lawsuit against King County and before the cases could go to trial, King County settled out-of-court. As it turned out, in 1984, the shattered Eleanore Rose would receive the sum of $112,000, and James Ott (husband of Janice Ott) would split the same amount with Janice's parents, Don and Ferold Blackburn. King County was never able to determine exactly what happened to the remains of Denise Naslund, Janice Ott, or the other victim. I remember reading years ago that someone had said a single employee, acting on his or her own, may have simply thrown them away.

NEIL, PETE

Occasionally, there are people who have a brush with something historic, or infamous, and they're only mentioned briefly. And such is the case with Pete Neil. Neil has the distinction of spending, along with two others, a last time of socializing with Lynda Ann Healy a mere six or seven hours before Ted Bundy entered the rooming house where Healy maintained a basement apartment, and swept her away forever.

According to police reports, Pete came over to the rooming house, located at 5517 12th Street N.E., and probably ate the dinner that Lynda Healy had prepared for others in the house. Afterward, Healy, Pete, Joanne Testa, and Ginger Heath, walked the couple of blocks to Dante's Tavern, where the four of them had first one pitcher of beer, and then another, all the while laughing, talking, and having a good time. And then, at around 9:00 p.m., or a little thereafter, they all walked back to the rooming house. Pete was needing to get back so he could catch the 9:41 bus back to his place. Once home, Pete Neil gathered up some records he'd left there and hurried out the door and headed for the bus stop.

NEARY, NITA

Nita Neary was a member of the Chi Omega sorority house in Tallahassee, Florida, when Bundy, in a homicidal rage, entered it in the early morning hours of January 15, 1978 with only murder on his mind. Neary had been on a date that night, and unbeknownst to her, as the car lights of her boyfriend's car shown on the rear of the house, the lights entered the back bedroom of Karen Chandler and Kathy Kleiner who had just been beaten severely by Bundy. Indeed, he hadn't yet finished with Karen Chandler (he attacked Kleiner first), and if he hadn't been startled by the lights, he might very well have killed them both, just as he had murdered Margaret Bowman and Lisa Levy only minutes before entering their room.

Bundy, still holding the bloody log - now missing a great deal of bark – understood he needed to go and quickly left room 8. Shrouded in almost total darkness, he quickly descended the steps, and when he reached the bottom, he hesitated only a few seconds before turning the door handle and slipping out the front door. Bundy had no idea he'd been seen by Neary, who was standing in the darkness and caught only a quick glimpse of the man and his profile. Because the individual was wearing a cap pulled down and was wrapped in a heavy coat, the only aspect of the man that she could get that would be very accurate, was his straight, and somewhat unusual nose.

Once Bundy went to trial for the murders at Chi Omega, Nita Neary, after being asked to identify the man she saw that early morning, pointed directly at Ted Bundy as he sat at the witness table. The spectacle, indeed, the entire trial was televised nationally, and when Neary singled out Bundy with her words and that pointing finger, Bundy became noticeably uncomfortable, and it may be that psychologically he felt he was being revealed for what he was, and there was nothing he could do about it.

NELSON, MELANIE

After Bundy departed the Chi Omega house, leaving two dead and two seriously injured behind, and the women began to awake to the tragedy that befell them, a sense of high anxiety and shock began to take hold. Not everyone came out of their rooms at the same time, and all who did were met with the police moving about, emergency medical technicians pushing gurneys, and crying and bewildered young women who'd been awakened to a nightmare and didn't yet understand what had happened to them. What follows is from *The Bundy Murders*:

At 3:35 A.M. (only about thirteen minutes after the first responders arrived), Officer Henry Newkirk of the Tallahassee Police Department entered the foyer of Chi Omega and walked upstairs, where he found near-pandemonium on the part of the young residents of the sorority. Not only had they been awakened to the knowledge that an assault on two of their friends had just occurred, but the whisking away of an unresponsive Lisa Levy only heightened their fears. Correctly gauging the scene as an evidence-gathering nightmare, he quickly began rounding up the distraught and crying women and leading them into an empty room. His reason for doing so, he explained later, was "to quell some of the extraneous wandering and commotion."

After getting the women settled into room 2, Newkirk had just begun questioning them as to what they may have seen or knew, when Chi O sister, Melanie Nelson, who was worried that Margaret Bowman had not come out of her room, asked Officer Newkirk to, *look into room 9 to make sure Margaret Bowman was alright since she had not exited her room.* Newkirk immediately turned on his heels and went into Bowman's room. What follows is from Officer Newkirk's official report: *This writer entered room 9 and immediately closed the door behind me once I observed blood on a pillow.* This was the second fatality to be discovered at Chi Omega.

NELSON, POLLY

Polly Nelson was Ted Bundy's from 1986 through his execution on January 24, 1989, and is the author of *Defending the Devil: My Story As Ted Bundy's Last Lawyer*. Nelson fought many difficult legal battles for three years in her effort to keep her client alive, and worked closely with Dr. Dorothy Otnow Lewis to that end. Their efforts, however, were unsuccessful in keeping Bundy out of the electric chair.

NEWKIRK, OFFICER HENRY

Officer Henry Newkirk was one of the officers responding to the brutal attack at the Chi Omega sorority house in Tallahassee, Florida, where Ted Bundy killed two and severely injured two. Newkirk arrived 13 minutes after the first responders were at the scene, and as soon as he walked the steps to the second floor he assessed the situation, and because activity on the second floor was now reaching the point of pandemonium (police officers, EMT's, and distraught women all practically bumping into one another), he took charge of the situation and had all the Chi O students follow him into an empty room 2. Just as he started to question them as to what they knew or saw, Melanie Nelson, a Chi O sister, asked him to check on Margaret Bowman as she hadn't yet exited her room. As Newkirk entered room 9, he saw blood on the pillow and immediately closed the door. Here he found Margaret Bowman both bloody and deceased. He would also examine the body of Lisa Levy located in room 4, as well as the carnage left behind in room 8 where Kathy Kleiner and Karen Chandler were attacked and severely injured.

NORMAN, DR. ART

Dr. Art Norman was a psychologist who worked with Bundy's defense team during the killer's final years of death row. Norman would later reveal that Bundy told him "in no uncertain terms", that his launch into murder occurred when he murdered two women while he was living in Philadelphia. This would be in 1969.

O'CONNELL, JOHN

John O'Connell was Ted Bundy's defense attorney in Utah after Bundy was charged with the abduction of Carol DaRonch in October 1975. O'Connell had an office at: 12 Exchange Place, Salt Lake City, Utah, 84111.

John O'Connell was a good lawyer who adhered to the letter of the law, and it can be said he did everything he could to exonerate his client, but Bundy, being actually guilty of the crime for which he'd been charged, was not going to survive his encounter with the Salt Lake City authorities unscathed. And it would be during the "bench" trial, where Judge Stewart Hansen, and not a jury, would decide Ted Bundy's fate for the kidnapping of Carol DaRonch. And after O'Connell did his best to dismantle the case the prosecution had built against his client, it would do no good. Bundy (who also assisted in his own defense) would be found guilty of the kidnaping of DaRonch and was sentenced to a term of one to fifteen years in the Utah State Prison.

OLIVERSON, DENISE

Denise Oliverson (1950-1975) fell victim to Ted Bundy on April 6, 1975, as she bicycled through the small community of Grand Junction, Colorado. They were on a collision course with each other, and it was all a matter of time and chance. True, Bundy was hunting for a victim, but that victim could have been anybody. He was trolling for a victim and his eyes were open to even the slightest opportunity that might present itself. And if he saw something he very much wanted, he would work very hard to get it. But no matter how it came about, they were destined to meet.

Although several stories have surfaced over the years since her murder, as to what she was doing just before she encountered Bundy and how she disappeared, the authorities do know that she had had an argument with her boyfriend, and that she left on her bicycle and headed to her parents' home in the northern section of the city. It's also likely Bundy initiated the attack either on or near a bridge which ran over the Colorado River as she traveled to her parents' home. And while Bundy never revealed exactly how he got her (it was most likely a swift attack using his crowbar as she peddled past his VW), he did admit to taking her onto I-70 heading west and that he stopped his VW before crossing the state line into Utah, killed her, and dumped her body in the Colorado River. The remains of Denise Oliverson has never been recovered.

OLYMPIA, WASHINGTON

Olympia, Washington, located 60 miles south west of Seattle, is the capitol of Washington State. Today (2019) it has a population of some 46,000, but when Ted Bundy was a figure in the city and was hunting and killing women in 1974, its population was roughly 25,000. Sitting only seven miles from downtown Olympia, is The Evergreen State College. And it would be here, on March 12, 1974, that Donna Manson would have a fatal encounter with Ted Bundy.

Donna had left her first-year-student dorm around 7:00 p.m., and headed out into the chilly and slightly drizzly night air. She took a trail that was common to her, that was shrouded in on both sides by tall thick fir trees (as are all the trails here at Evergreen State), and her walk should have taken her no more than a few minutes to reach the library where a jazz concert was about to start on the first floor. However, there's no sign that she even reached the outside of the building, so it may be that Bundy either met her on the trail, offered some ruse, or attacked her. Less likely, is that he met her on the outside of the library, and convinced her to leave with him from there. Her remains were never recovered.

ONDRAK, DETECTIVE DARYLE M.

Detective Daryle M. Ondrak (1930-1988) was a homicide detective with the Salt Lake County Sheriff's Office., and would encounter Ted Bundy the first time after Bundy was stopped in the early morning hours of August 16, 1975 in Granger, Utah. He'd been stopped by Utah Highway Patrol officer, Robert Hayward, who radioed the Salt Lake County Sheriff's Office who sent a patrol car with two officers, and Detective Ondrak was dispatched to the scene as well.

When Ondrak saw the gym bag Bundy had in the car, with the contents of rope, electrical cord, as well as other odd implements spilling out, he knew these were more than burglar's tools (what he was being charged with carrying), because some of what he had was for tying people up. Later, when speaking with Detective Jerry Thompson about Bundy he referred to him as "strange man." When Thompson asked him what he meant by strange, Ondrak said, "I used to be in the Marine Corps... You meet a lot of strange people in the Corps. I don't know. It's just a gut reaction. This man's into something big."

OREGON STATE UNIVERSITY

Oregon State University, in Corvallis, Oregon, plays a unique part in the Ted Bundy story, as it was from here (for the full story, see: Parks, Kathy) that he, by way of a ruse, led Kathy Parks away from the cafeteria in the Memorial Union Commons close to 11:00 p.m. on May 6, 1974. Once out of the area, he later told a writer, he took control of her and transported her back to Washington State, where he murdered her.

O'REILY, KEVIN

Kevin O'Reily became Ted Bundy's attorney after his first escape from Colorado, as his own attorneys were now witnesses to his crime of escape and would now be called now testify against him. It also meant they could not represent him. Of course, Bundy would insist with participating with his own defense, and it would be a point of frustration for O'Reily; and it would be this way with Bundy's Florida attorneys as well.

OTT, JAMES

James Ott was the husband of Janice Ott, and it's clear that he loved his wife, and her abduction and murder at the hands of Ted Bundy must have turned his life into a nightmare. That said, it is also clear that the couple did not have a traditional union, and James Ott would tell police the same thing. What follows is from his official statement to King County authorities:

Legally, I was Jan's husband. However, we liked to keep our marriage out of its traditional role. That is, being devoted only to each other, such that either of us could not expand ourselves in our work and with other people. We both felt a need to have an independence of our own, so that we could expand and in turn, enhance our relationship.

Ott doesn't explain the rules of their relationship beyond what is written here. And their current separation appears to be the result only of James Ott attending medical school in California while Janice worked in her career as a Seattle probation and parole officer. And they were in regular contact with each other by phone. In fact, the couple spoke by phone the night before her disappearance, at 10:00 p.m. on Saturday, July 13, 1974.

OTT, JANICE

Janice Ott

Janice Ott (1951-1974) was Ted Bundy's first victim at Lake Sammamish on July 14, 1974. That Sunday morning, Janice had washed and dried her clothes at the Suds Shop Laundromat which sits (even in 2019) just across the street from the little apartment she rented at 75 Front Street. While there, she had a conversation with the owner, David Allison McKibben. McKibben, who was in the process of finishing up his work, asked Ott if she wanted to get a cup of coffee at a nearby restaurant, and she said yes. After coffee, the two went their separate ways, and within a short time, Janice would bicycle to Lake Sammamish State Park. And it was here, soon after she got settled on a towel and began putting on sunscreen, that Bundy came up to her and asked her to help him with a sail boat at his parent's house up in Issaquah. After a brief conversation (which was heard by others near to them), Janice Ott gathered up her things and left with Bundy, walking her yellow 10-speed bike alongside her. Later, Bundy would tell FBI agent, William

"Bill" Hagmaier, that he kept Janice Ott alive for hours, so that later in the afternoon, Janice Ott would see Bundy arrive with Denise Naslund. And eventually, he would murder one in front of the other.

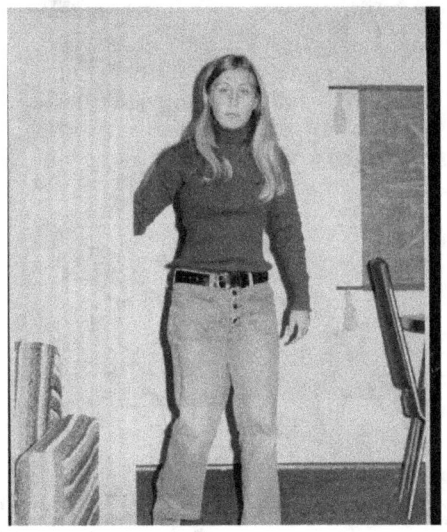

Janice Ott

PALUMBO, HENRY

Henry Palumbo was one of two men returning to The Oak around 4:00 a.m. only about an hour after the attack on Chi Omega. As they approached the home, they saw Bundy and greeted him. But Bundy, who was staring blankly in the direction of the university, oddly did not answer or acknowledge them. Palumbo, along with his friend, Russell Gage, would later testify at Bundy's Chi Omega trial.

PARKS, KATHY

Kathy Parks

In 1974, Kathy Parks (1954-1974), originally from California, was a student at Oregon State University in Corvallis, Oregon. And it would be here, a little before 11:00 p.m. on May 6, 1974, that she would encounter Ted Bundy in the Memorial Union Commons cafeteria. And because it was closing at 11:00, besides a worker or two milling about, Bundy and Parks may have been the only two people still there. It seems certain no one noticed them, and her disappearance would remain a bit of a mystery for a number of years until Bundy conveyed to a writer in the third-person that Parks may have encountered her abductor in the cafeteria. He then spoke of convincing her to leave with him, and once the opportunity presented itself, he took control of her.

Later, investigators would interview Lorraine Fargo who stopped to speak with Kathy on the corner that is just across the narrow side street that runs beside the Memorial Union Commons. Lorraine was aware of the issues Kathy was having with her boyfriend (he wanted to settle down, she didn't), and she asked her to come back to her room in Sackett Hall, but Kathy didn't want to just yet. She wanted to walk around the campus, she told Lorraine, but promised to come over in a little while. As Lorraine watched Kathy cross the narrow street, she dropped a letter into the mail box. That letter, postmarked May 7, 1974, was addressed to her boyfriend, Christy McPhee, telling him that she loved him and was looking forward to seeing him. She ended it by saying:

I'm feeling down right now, due to a combination of things, I suppose. To tell you the truth, I don't even feel like finishing this letter. I think I'll go walk around outside a while. I'm sorry this is such a bum letter. I really am. But, after all, everyone has their ups and downs. This day has especially had its share of bad news. Well – I'm looking forward to seeing you – very much. When you come, please put your arms around me and make me feel like everything is O.K. I really miss you. I'm needing the comfort of your presence now.

I love you,
Kathy

Bundy most likely kept Parks alive, tied up and gagged, for the 250-mile trip back to Washington State, where he soon killed her and dumped her remains on Taylor Mountain.

PARMENTER, DANNY

Danny Parmenter is the brother of Leslie Parmenter, who was an almost Ted Bundy victim on February 8, 1978. Danny played a big part in saving Leslie at a critical moment when this author believes the abduction was about to take place. For the full story, see below.

PARMENTER, LESLIE

Leslie Parmenter, who, at age 14, barely escaped from Ted Bundy in a K-Mart parking lot in Jacksonville. Florida on February 8, 1978. This photograph of Leslie was taken one year later.

Leslie Parmenter was only 14-years-old when she had an encounter with Ted Bundy on February 8, 1978, in Jacksonville, Florida. Bundy, who was no longer the refined killer he'd been in Northwest, was by now often physically dirty and unkempt, and was no longer drawing women to him. As such, his venture into Jacksonville where he was most likely hunting for college-aged women but was unsuccessful, turned his attention to someone much younger (as he'd done before), when he spotted Leslie Parmenter walking along the side parking lot road that runs along K-Mart's windowless side. It was an abduction that quickly failed, however, when Leslie's brother, Danny Parmenter, drove up in his truck. I had the pleasure of interviewing Leslie Parmenter (I was the first American writer to do so) in January 2019, and her story appears in my book, *Ted Bundy's Murderous Mysteries*, published in April 2019.

PATCHEN, DETECTIVE DONALD

Det. Donald Patchen, lead investigator for the Tallahassee PD into the Chi Omega murders of January 15, 1978.

Detective Donald Patchen, of the Tallahassee, PD, was the lead investigator for the Chi Omega murders of January 1978. Patchen's first meeting with Bundy would be in Pensacola after Bundy's arrest there in the early morning hours of February 15, 1978. The reason why Tallahassee law enforcement was called into a Pensacola arrest was because Bundy had in his possession a number of stolen credit cards, and some of these had been lifted from Florida State University students. As such, representatives from the Leon County Sheriff's Office (Steve Bodiford) and the Tallahassee Police Department (Don Patchen), soon hit the road together and traveled to Pensacola where Pensacola Police Department Detective Norman Chapman awaited them. And when it became clear that Ted Bundy may in fact be involved in the Chi Omega murders, and the probability that he was responsible for the killing of 12-year-old Kimberly

Diane Leach, he was transferred to a specially reinforced maximum-security cell in the Leon County Jail.

On January 23, 1989, Don Patchen got a call from a man who said they had one more seat open for Bundy's execution, scheduled for the next day. Patchen, a combat vet from the Vietnam War, and a tough homicide cop, said yes, he'd take that seat. Patchen was scheduled to meet the governor of Florida the next morning for breakfast, but because he'd accepted the spot to witness Bundy's execution, he called to postpone their meeting. The next morning, as Don Patchen entered the small room that separates them from the execution chamber only by a wall and partition of glass, Bundy spotted Patchen and waved. When I interviewed Don in 2008 for my book, *The Bundy Murders*, I asked him if watching the execution was difficult for him. He told me no, and quickly explained he'd seen so much death, first in Vietnam and then as a detective, that watching a terrible person like Bundy die was nothing at all.

PAYNE, OFFICER GERALD

Officer Gerald Payne was the first to arrive (along with his partner, Officer Mitch Miller) to the duplex at 431-A on Dunwoody Street in Tallahassee, Florida. It was the home of FSU student Cheryl Thomas and they knew something was very wrong. Her neighbor at 431-B, Debbie Ciccarelli, had reported to police she had heard "loud pounding" in the apartment, and that it sounded like her friend, Cheryl Thomas, was crying and pleading with someone. And because Cheryl hadn't responded to Debbie pounding on the thin separating wall and the yelling for her to respond, and because she wouldn't answer her phone when Debbie called her, she telephoned the Tallahassee Police Department.

Unbeknownst to Debbie Ciccarelli, the Tallahassee PD, as well as the Leon County Sheriff's Office, had their hands full over at the Chi Omega sorority house some four or five blocks away. The sorority house had been attacked only an hour earlier, leaving two dead and two seriously injured. Even so, patrol cars from both departments raced to the scene. Officer Payne and two other officers had been looking for a way into the apartment, and were about to break the front door when Ciccarelli came out her front door and offered the officers a key Cheryl had given to her.

PED LINE MEDICAL SUPPLIES

In the fall of 1970, Ted Bundy was hired by Ped Line Medical Supplies as a delivery driver. He would stay with the company for the next five months. During that time, he would pilfer a number of medical items from plaster-of-Paris to a speculum; the same device found rammed into the vagina of Karen Sparks (identified in my book, *The Bundy Murders,* as Terri Caldwell) when he attacked her in her rooming house sometime after 2:00 a.m. on January 4, 1974. Sparks was also severely beaten about the head and face with a blunt object as well.

Of course, Bundy intended to kill her and no doubt believed she was breathing her last breaths as he left her below-ground quarters and headed out into the night. It is believed that this attack was the first of what this writer believes was Bundy's launch into full-time murder in the first month of 1974. When she didn't die, it's likely he determined to never make that mistake again, as his next victim, Lynda Ann Healy, was attacked in her rooming house as she slept, rendered unconscious, and carried out into the night.

Karen Sparks would be in a coma for ten days and the hospital for 30, and it is believed she did not make a complete recovery, as victims of such severe beatings often have residual issues that must be managed.

PENSACOLA, FLORIDA

Had Ted Bundy been able to look into his future, say, when he was whisking Lynda Healy away from her rooming house in the early morning hours of February 1, 1974, he would have seen that Pensacola, Florida would be his end of the road.

Having created a firestorm of investigation in the city of Tallahassee with first the attack on the Chi Omega sorority house in the early morning hours of January 15, 1978, and a new investigation from Lake City, with the disappearance of 12-year-old Kimberly Diane Leach, Bundy knew it was time to flee. But here Bundy would have trouble. Bundy was prone to dawdling, and was doing so in the early morning hours of February 15, 1978 – exactly one month to the day after the attack on Chi Omega.

Bundy could have easily cleared the Florida state line, but instead, was spotted by Pensacola patrol officer David Lee sitting in an orange (and stolen) VW Bug behind a closed restaurant. Suspicious, Lee hit his lights and Bundy took off. After a few minutes, Bundy knew he couldn't get away and pulled to the side of the road. However, it would not be an easy arrest, and Bundy would fight with Lee. For the full story, see: Lee, Officer David

PHILADELPHIA, PENNSYLVANIA

Philadelphia, Pennsylvania, would be the place where Bundy would, in later years, have his first memories. Of course, before it was home to little Teddy Cowell, it was home to his mother Louise, her sisters, and her parents. Ted's grandfather, it's been believed, was a violent man, and had a stash of pornography that his grandson would peruse at will. Bundy's early life is heavy on rumors about Samuel Cowell and how he may have effected Bundy's upbringing, with little known facts to back it up. However, it would be here in Philadelphia, before Louise took the child to Washington

State to start a new life, that her sisters would see odd things from the child, and two incidents do stand out.

One event occurred early one morning when one of the aunts found that Bundy had placed some kitchen knives pointing at her in her bed. Apparently, the boy said nothing but just stared at her. Another time happened when the aunt (it's unknown by this writer if this is the same aunt who experienced the knives in her bed, or another sister of Louise), but as the boy stood on a railway station platform with the aunt around dusk, she said his personality began to change right in front of her, and she found it both noticeable and disturbing.

PITKIN COUNTY COURTHOUSE

The Pitkin County Courthouse, located on East Main Street in Aspen, Colorado, was built in 1890 and continues to function as a courthouse today. And while it's a commanding structure, and was added to the National Register of Historic Places in 1975, it would be Ted Bundy and his association with the old courthouse that would propel it into the national spotlight. More appropriately, it would be his bold escape from the courthouse on June 7, 1977, while he was on trial for the murder of Caryn Campbell, that would be seared into the minds of the public, not just in Aspen, but everywhere the news media carried it.

Because Bundy was, as usual, assisting in his own defense, he had been using the law library on the second floor on a regular basis. And because Bundy was, as usual, being folksy with everyone and completely non-threatening, the guards assigned to keep their prisoner secure, were not always doing so. And Bundy, who'd been scheming of ways to escape, noticed how often they were leaving the windows wide open on the second floor. Without question, he had to have gone over to the window (and perhaps on more than one occasion) and peered out to try and imagine how well he'd fare in a jump from that location. It would not be an easy jump, as it's a 25 foot drop from the window's ledge (because the basement rises a half floor above ground, it's a two and a half story building, making it a 25 foot drop), but Bundy figured he could manage the fall without injuring himself, and he was mostly correct. During his jump on that sunny June morning, Bundy did slightly injure his leg, but it was in no way a real hindrance to him, and he would remain free for almost a week before he was recaptured.

PLISCHKE, JACQUELINE

Jacqueline Plischke had an encounter with Ted Bundy at Lake Sammamish on July 14, 1974. She had arrived at the park around 4:00 p.m. Bundy, who had led Janice Ott away from the park before noon, was now back seeking another victim. As soon as Plischke arrived, she locked up her bike on the rack where all the other bikes were parked. According to the record, she wore, "blue jeans, sort of cut-offs, and a pink, very brief bikini top." What follows is a portion of her statement, given to detectives on July17, 1974:

On Sunday, July 14, 1974, at about 4 p.m., I arrived at Lake Sammamish State Park on my bicycle. I was there for about twenty minutes. I had gone to the point on the beach where they water ski from. I was approached by a white male, early twenties, 5'8", medium build, dark blond hair, hair length was about to the middle of his ear, average skin tone, left arm in a sling and sling was beige in color. The sling was not neat, something, either a cast or wrap was over his arm. He had a wide face, average features and his speech was smooth. He talked clearly, no slang words – everything was distinct. The first thing he said was, "Hello, I was wondering if you could help me put my sailboat on my car?" I said, "I'm not very strong." He said, "It's better that I asked someone who was alone." He answered my comments right away. I said, "I'm waiting for someone." He then seemed to not have any interest in me." He said, "Oh, I see." Then he turned away and walked toward the bath house. I was about two feet from him. About fifteen minutes prior to talking with him, I had seen the same guy look at me when I came in. I just noticed his face and sling at that time. I was riding my bicycle. I was wearing blue jeans, sort of cut-offs, and a pink, very brief bikini top. About ten minutes after he left from talking with me, I looked at my watch and it was 4:30 p.m. I did not see him again. He did not act nervous. He was not pushy. He didn't seem disappointed when I told him I was waiting for someone.

POCATELLO, IDAHO

Pocatello, Idaho plays a distinct role in the Ted Bundy murders, for it's one of two places where we know beyond doubt Bundy murdered a 12-year-old child (the other is Lake City, Florida where he murdered Kimberly Diane Leach, also 12). Not only did he murder a young girl, but he would change his MO of murder while there as well.

On May 5, 1975, Ted Bundy, having already gassed up his VW, headed north on I-15. His destination was Pocatello, only 165 miles— a short trip for someone like Bundy. His reason for this northern trip was once again murder. He'd been killing outside of Utah since the first of the year (three known victims in Colorado, but certainly others) as the manhunt in Utah made killing there almost impossible. But Pocatello had no manhunt to run from, and the Idaho authorities had no idea that Bundy killed a hitchhiker that he'd picked up outside of Boise on September 2, 1974 as he was moving to Salt Lake City to attend law school.

Bundy's target for hunting women would focus on Idaho State University; at least that's where he thought he'd find a victim. But, as I discovered during my research for *The Bundy Murders*, it was still cold in Pocatello, and for the two days Bundy was there, snow showers periodically blanketed the city. Women were not going to stop for Bundy, even if he was hobbling on crutches or had his arm in a sling, while he displayed his difficulty carrying books. And his one attempt indoors occurred when he took an elevator to an upper floor of the women's dormitory building on campus, and he was stopped by a male employee and asked to provide identification. Bundy said he didn't have any and was immediately asked to leave.

Without question, Bundy believed that by the end of that day-evening hunt, he would have the one he came for, but that didn't happen. However, the next day, he would leave his room at the Holiday Inn, get into his car and begin yet another hunt, and most likely he turned right on the road that runs in front of the hotel. Not knowing where he was going, he kept on a straight shot – first on Pocatello Creek Road which runs into East Alameda which runs into West Alameda, until he found himself in front of Alameda Middle School at lunchtime as the kids were streaming out the door.

Bundy spotted one of these children, 12-year-old Lynette Culver, and waved her over to his car. Bundy never explained what he said to get her into his VW, but he did tell authorities what they discussed on the way to the hotel, and because of this, investigators were convinced Bundy was her killer. In any event, once inside the hotel room, Bundy took control of her, and in what was a change in his MO (strangling his victims while having sex with them from behind), he drowned young Lynette in the bathtub. Being a necrophile, Bundy also admitted having sex with Lynette's dead body. Between 2:30 and 3:00 p.m., Bundy would dump her body into the Snake River some five miles north of Pocatello. Now satiated, he would return to Salt Lake City and his second-floor apartment at 565 First Avenue.

PORTER, OFFICER DONALD

On the evening of February 19, 1978, Officer Donald Porter was one of two officers posted to keep an eye out for any suspicious activity in the area surrounding Dunwoody Street where Bundy attacked Cheryl Thomas almost one month earlier. These kinds of assignments can be exceedingly boring and can appear a complete waste of time. They can also pay off. And just so the reader may understand what happened here, I will describe the layout of this area of the Florida State University.

Stadium Drive runs south, and then east past the Doak Campbell Stadium and when it reached the front of the structure, it becomes University Avenue and that in turn follows the configuration of the stadium and heads north. As it begins University and then rounds the loop to head north, West St. Augustine intersects with University, and one block north of here, W. Pensacola intersects with University. And it would be here that Ted Bundy would encounter those desperately trying to catch him.

At approximately 10:45 p.m., Bundy, having "rounded" the stadium, was on foot walking north on the sidewalk on Stadium Drive, and as he turned right onto West St. Augustine, he noticed a patrol car facing away from him. Bundy immediately took "evasive action" according to Officer Roy Dickey who spotted him in his rearview mirror (Dickey was parked where Dunwoody intersects with St. Augustine, and Bundy was close and heading straight towards this location), and as he would write in his report, the individual quickly cut across the street and went between two houses in his attempt to get to W. Pensacola one block north. Dickey immediately radioed Officer Donald Porter who was also in his vehicle and parked on Pensacola, but about a block east of where Bundy would have come out from between the two houses. A quick check, however, revealed Bundy never made it out the other side, and that was the last time he was sighted. After Bundy's arrest, Dickey would positively identify Ted Bundy as the man he saw take evasive action that night.

PRICE, UTAH

In the early morning hours (between 3:30 and 4:00 a.m.) of January 28, 1977, Colorado investigator, Michael Fisher, took possession of Ted Bundy to transfer him from the Utah State Prison to the jail in Aspen, Colorado so he could stand trial for the murder Caryn Campbell, whom Bundy had led away from the Wildwood Inn in Snowmass, Colorado, on January 12, 1975 and murdered.

Bundy was placed in the backseat of an unmarked patrol car with Mike Fisher sitting beside him. In front of Bundy, sitting in the passenger seat was Undersheriff Ben Meyers, and the driver was Deputy Rick Kralicek. The three lawmen and their prisoner drove off into the night, and within a few minutes, they were headed south on I-15 and once they came to Spanish Fork, they took Highway 6 until they entered Price, Utah, where the four men had breakfast at a mom and pop diner. Mike Fisher would later tell this author that, just as Bundy remained silent on the drive, he would remain quiet here as well. Fisher did say he would periodically look over at him and the others; and the investigator also stated he believes that Bundy was fearful during the ride as he believed that while they traveled those dark back roads, they might just decide to act as judge, jury and executioner and be done with him. Instead, Mike Fisher delivered him safely to Aspen later that day.

PROVO, UTAH

Provo, Utah is home to Brigham Young University, and it would be here, in the fading light of June 27, 1975, that Susan Curtis, 15, would encounter Ted Bundy, who would at that moment attack her and render her unconscious, or, more likely, stop and speak with her, and by ruse, lead her away to a spot where he could overwhelm and capture her. For the full story, see Curtis, Susan, in this book.

RAFFERTY, CHERYL

Cheryl Rafferty was a student at Florida State University who encountered Bundy (he was in the midst of attacking her) in the early evening of January 14, 1978, only hours before he entered the Chi Omega in the early morning hours of January 15th to commit murder and mayhem. According to the incident report she filed with FSU campus police, she had just gotten out of her car when a man jumped out from behind a bush (something Bundy used to do for fun with women he wanted to frighten back in Washington State). Because Rafferty spotted him immediately, she picked up her pace and saw her stalker do the same. Understanding the situation was turning dangerous, the young woman now broke into a full run, as did the man. Fortunately, she made it to the safety of Reynolds Hall, and the man was forced to let her go. Later, after being shown pictures of Ted Bundy, she identified him as her attacker.

RANCOURT, SUSAN ELAINE

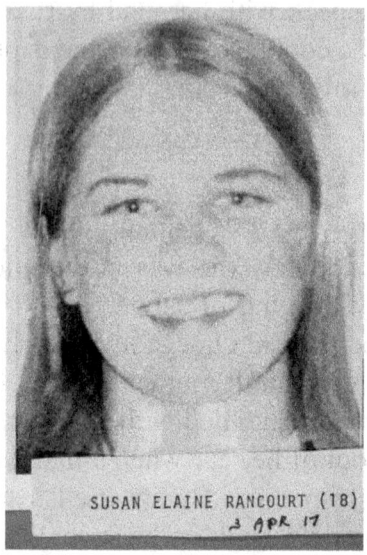

Susan Rancourt

Susan Rancourt (1955-1974) disappeared from Central Washington State College (CWSC) on April 17, 1974. While we don't know everything about her abduction, there is much we do know, both about her actions that night, and the actions of Ted Bundy. On this night, Susan placed clothes in the washing machine, and also attended a meeting for those wanting to be dorm counselors. Bundy, who had been hunting since the early afternoon around the library, but without success, encountered Susan around 10:00 p.m. while playing the injured man with a sling on his arm fumbling books. Susan, obviously not suspecting a thing, agreed to help him, and Bundy led her to a remote area on the edge of campus, with little light and no other people nearby. At this point, Bundy would have waylaid her with a blow from a crowbar that he'd placed underneath the car, possibly behind the rear passenger side tire, and quickly hoisted her into the floor of the car, because we know Bundy was removing the passenger seat at this time. Unconscious,

Susan would take the short drive on I-90 to Issaquah, where Bundy would take her about 200 yards up an old logging road and kill her. However, he would not leave her there. The skull of Susan Rancourt was found with three other skulls (or parts of skulls) on Taylor Mountain. Taylor was primarily a dump site for the heads of his victims only.

The area at CWSC where Bundy parked his car and led Susan Rancourt to it on the night of April 17, 1974 and abducted her after knocking her out with a crowbar. The train trestle at CWSC (where his VW was parked) crossed this road at an angle approximately where the red car is located. Bundy and his first potential victim, as well as victim Susan Rancourt, came from the left of the picture, having crossed the small bridge and Black Hall which is also on the left and not shown in this picture. The trail they took would have caused them to enter the area about where the asphalt separates the concrete sidewalk on the left of the photo. It's important to note that the buildings in the foreground were not there in 1974, making it perhaps the most secluded area on campus.

RANKIN, ELZA E.

Elza Rankin was hunting grouse with a friend on September 7, 1974 when they discovered the partial remains of Janice Ott and Denise Naslund. What follows is a portion of his official statement given to police:

I, Elza Everett Rankin 1-6-1904 of 11717 25th Ave. N.E. Seattle... give this statement to Off. C.M. Wilson Issaquah P.D. My friend & I (Elsie Hammond) arrived in this area to do some grouse hunting at about 7:00 a.m. 8-2-74. We drove around the woods for about 2 – 2 ½ hours. At about 9:30 Elsie stated he wanted to do some more hunting. I waited at the car for him to return. He returned approx 15 minutes later. Elsie stated he had found a human skull. We both went with another lad back to where he had seen the skull. I first saw the hair about twenty feet from where the skull was. I then saw some type of rib section ½ way from hair to skull. Then we went to look at the skull. We then went back to our car & Elsie went to report what we found.

Had Rankin and Hammond not been hunting that day, the remains of Janice Ott and Denise Naslund may have gone unnoticed for a very long time, if not forever.

REICHERT, DAVE

Dave Reichert, who has had a storied career in both law enforcement and politics in Washington State, played a part in the Ted Bundy story when he worked alongside Investigator Robert Keppel on what is known as the Green River Task Force. Bundy had offered his help to catch the killer (later identified as Gary Ridgway), and Keppel saw it as an opportunity to soften up the Bundy who might later agree to talk with him about his Washington murders, and both Reichert and Keppel began the process of interviewing the incarcerated killer. Reichert also wrote a book about his experiences, *Chasing the Devil: My Twenty-Year Quest to Capture the Green River Killer*.

RENEAU, RUSS

Russ Reneau, chief investigator for the Idaho Attorney General's office, was informed only days before Ted Bundy's execution that the killer was wanting to confess to two murders in the state of Idaho. One case that immediately came to mind was the May 6, 1975 disappearance of 12-year-old Lynette Culver, who strangely vanished from Alameda Middle School in Pocatello, Idaho. Lots of rumors surrounded the disappearance, but nothing of actual substance that would lead investigators to an answer. As such, Reneau would have plenty of questions about this case, and he wondered if Bundy had anything to do with it. The trip to see the confessing killer would be a search for truth, and to that end, Russ Reneau, Randy Everitt and Jim Whitehead gathered all their materials together and boarded a flight for Florida. What follows is a small portion taken from my book, *The Trail of Ted Bundy: Digging Up the Untold Stories*:

During my October 2015 telephone call to Russ Reneau, I asked him about Bundy's demeanor and attitude while they were there, and whether Bundy had looked at him eye-to-eye. He said Bundy was very tired, and that he did look them in the eyes while talking about things in a general sense. But as he described the murders, he would look away, as if he were concentrating. He also said that as Bundy talked about the abduction and murder of Lynette Culver, he became noticeably focused on what he was saying. At the beginning of the interview, Bundy was the first one to speak. Although he seemed a bit disjointed, Russ said, it was clear he was ready to get down to business and make the confessions. What follows is the transcript of Bundy beginning the interview:

All right, let's begin with... try to focus in on the date here... the period. I believe it's April 1975, possibly May. It's in one of those two months. I traveled from Salt Lake

City to... now here is my confusion to either Pocatello or Idaho Falls and I tend to think it was Pocatello but I'm not absolutely sure. Trying to recall perhaps the day of the week... again I know it was during the week, not on a weekend. I stayed in a Holiday Inn in, well in all likelihood Pocatello... for at least one night. I'm cutting down on a lot of factual stuff right now... you're free to ask. Just to give you the picture. I abducted a young girl from a junior high school, probably in Pocatello.

By the time the interview concluded exactly one hour later, they had a lot of information that investigators would now try to confirm, if possible, a credible link between Ted Bundy and the disappearance of Lynette Culver. And after discussing Bundy's claims with her family and certain people at her school, it was determined that Bundy was in fact responsible for her abduction and murder.

ROBERTS, JENNIFER

Jennifer Roberts was a friend of Georgann Hawkins, and in fact, it was Jennifer, on the last night of Georgann's life, that had walked with her to the party that evening so they could unwind a bit with friends and have a couple of beers. By about 2:30 a.m., June 11, 1974, they returned to the alley behind Greek Row. Here they parted as Jennifer walked on down the alley while Georgann, knowing someone dangerous to women was out there, watched her safely arrive at the spot where she could then enter their sorority house. They called out to each other one last time, and as Jennifer turned to enter her sorority, Georgann went into her boyfriend's fraternity house by entering the back door that leads to the alley.

ROBERTSON, SHELLEY

Shelley Robertson (1951-1975), 23, disappeared from Golden, Colorado on July 1, 1975. The first alert for her family that something was wrong is when she didn't show up for work in the family's printing business that morning. Almost one month later, on August 23rd, her naked and decomposing body was found at the bottom of a mineshaft in Berthoud Pass, some 40 miles from Golden. She had been bound with duct tape, and apparently, police were unable to find any finger prints on the tape. Indeed, no evidence was recovered at the scene that could point to anyone.

Because Ted Bundy was a creature of habit, and because he'd stopped in Golden twice very recently, he cannot be ruled out as a suspect. The case is considered unsolved and remains officially open.

ROBINSON, SHERIFF RON

Sheriff Ronald (Ron) Robinson (1926-2007), was sheriff of Summit County, Utah from 1962-1982, and would play a part in the Bundy case in 1974 when the body of Melissa Smith, 18, was located in Summit County. Bundy, who had a habit of sometimes leaving bodies purposely close to civilization, did so with the body of Melissa Smith. What follows is a portion taken from the official report of the Salt Lake County Sheriff's Office, and mentions Summit County Sheriff Robinson's role and the exact location where Melissa's body was found. Keep in mind that as the detectives surrounded the body and the investigation began, no one had any idea that they were viewing the remains of Melissa Smith, the daughter of Midvale, Utah chief of police, Louis Smith:

Victim: Smith, Melissa
Address: 180 Fern Drive, Midvale, Utah
ELEMENTS OF INVESTIGATION:

Body of a young white female American found on a hillside in the oak brush east of Summit Park Subdivision in conditions which would lead investigating officers to believe that this is an obvious homicide. Mountainside covered in oak brush.

WEAPONS USED: One navy blue sock used for the purpose of strangulation; some type of blunt instrument, possibly a rock.

Discovered by PHILLIP D. HUGHES. Further details on Mr. Hughes are contained in Sheriff Ron Robinson's report. It [the victim's body] was found by Mr. Hughes in the location described in item #3.

At approximately 4:00 p.m. on 10-27-74, this reporting officer received a phone call from Sheriff Ron Robinson of Summit County informing me that he had a homicide on his hands and that the nude body of a young white female American had been found on a hillside east of Summit Park Subdivision by some deer hunters. At this he requested my assistance at the scene. He also informed me that he had attempted to contact Capt. Hayward through the office but had been unsuccessful. I informed Sheriff Robinson that I would respond to the scene and make attempts to contact Capt. Hayward. After I hung up the phone from talking to Sheriff Robinson, I called Capt. Hayward's residence and he had already been informed of the situation, and he himself was en route to the scene. We agreed to meet at the Skyline Café at the Summit Park Subdivision. When we arrived at the Skyline Café in Summit Park, we were met by Sheriff Robinson and some of his deputies and were led into the scene of the actual crime.

ROCK SPRINGS, WYOMING

On Friday, March 14, 1975, and after having gassed up his fuel-efficient VW Beetle, he headed out of Salt Lake City on I-80. He was on yet another road trip to Colorado, and it was not for casual sight-seeing. His plan was to murder another Colorado woman. Bundy's usual MO as it pertains to geographic locations, was to keep hunting almost exclusively in the same state until the manhunt for him became so overwhelming that he had to leave the state for hunting trips in areas where no women were missing. This is what happened after he killed so many in Washington State that he had to move to Salt Lake City, Utah so he could begin the carnage there. And after Utah became too unsafe for him to operate, he branched out to neighboring Colorado, and he murdered his first victim in that state, a young nurse from Michigan, Caryn Campbell, on March 12, 1975. Because she was just the first murder he committed in the state, Bundy didn't expect to have any trouble dodging the authorities as they searched for a mad killer of women. And later, only after Bundy had been identified as the primary suspect in the cases of many missing and murdered women, would they obtain his gasoline purchases throughout the region, and it would be determined that for this trip, his first stop was in Rock Springs, Wyoming where he purchased gas. He may also have gotten something to eat, but there was no way for police to track him through the use of a regular credit card. Bundy's only form of credit, apparently, was his Chevron gas credit card.

ROGERS, ERNST AND FRIEDA

Ernst and Frieda Rogers were owners of a home at 4143 12th Street N.E. in Seattle. Bundy maintained a residence here from 1969 until he moved to Utah in September 1974. During these years he got to know the Rogers quite well, and the Rogers liked Bundy and were as shocked as anybody when detectives began visiting them in 1975 making their inquiries.

ROSE, GREG

Greg Rose was a radio host on a Portland, Oregon radio station in 1974, and got to know Lynda Ann Healy through both their on-air and off-air conversations when she'd call him every morning from her station to give them the ski reports. What follows is a portion of my interview with Greg and published in *The Bundy Secrets: Hidden Files on America's Worst Serial Killer*:

In 1974, Greg Rose was a disc jockey at KJIB 99.5 FM in Portland, Oregon. Each morning, and twice more throughout the day, KJIB would receive live on-air updates from Northwest Ski Promotions in Seattle, detailing conditions in commercial ski areas in their neck of the woods, including Mt. Hood, Mt. Bachelor, Mt. Baker, and Snoqualmie Pass for the station's listeners venturing in search for the perfect slope. As the midday deejay, Rose answered the late morning call from Northwest Ski Promotions, which is how he became acquainted with Lynda Ann Healy, one of Northwest's correspondents and a senior at the University of Washington, who spent her weekday mornings reciting the ski reports from across the region. Through this crossing of paths, via telephone, Greg Rose and Lynda Ann Healy got to know each other. Although they never met in person, as Greg related to me in an email, he "spoke to her frequently on the phone, and we sometimes exchanged 'snappy patter' between ourselves prior to the report." It was clear from his email, and our phone conversation later that week, that he and Lynda shared a cordial and professional rapport. Rose regrets that he never had the opportunity to travel to Seattle, for they had talked about meeting for a cup of coffee; a meeting that would have allowed them to put a face to the voice each had come to know over the phone.

On Thursday morning, January 31, 1974, Greg and Lynda were having their usual conversation prior to the live report she delivered on KJIB. The weekend was fast approaching, and Greg, making conversation, asked her what she was planning to do over the weekend. She had "stuff" to do, she told him, errands to run, and of course, the constant studying. It was all so very normal. When they said goodbye for the day, neither he nor Lynda had any idea what was about to transpire, especially that this would be their last conversation.

During our phone conversation in 2016, Greg told me that as soon as he learned she was missing, he knew it had to be foul play. Even so, it would be a long time before he would learn she was a victim of the serial killer, Ted Bundy.

ROSELLINI, ALBERT

Albert Rosellini (1910-2011) was a well-liked Democrat Washington State politician whose career spanned some 40 years; including two terms as governor 1957-1965. Born in Tacoma to Italian immigrant parents, he would become a state senator in 1939 (his first political position) and he would hold this office until he was elected governor in 1957. In 1972, he would try for a third term as governor, but was defeated. Bundy, an up and coming Republican campaigner, had been assigned to follow Rosellini around and report back everything deemed important to their campaign against him. This was the first time Bundy used a false mustache and may even have used a wig.

ROSS, TONY

Tony Ross was a friend of Donna Manson, and his name turns up briefly in the investigation of her disappearance from Evergreen State College on March 12, 1974. According to the report, once Donna was reported missing, Donna's parents, Lyle and Marie Manson were contacted by campus security. Lyle Manson, a music teacher in the Seattle public school system, got into his car and headed straight for Evergreen State College.

Upon arrival, Mr. Manson, along with the head of security, Gary Russell, and another individual, went into Donna's room to see if anything there could lead them to Donna, but nothing looked out of place. There were dollars and change on the counter. Her suitcases were there. Nothing pointed to her intentionally leaving, and it was not a good sign.

While there, Tony Ross stopped by to pick up an oil painting that belonged to him. Lyle Manson gave him the okay, and before he left, Ross, trying to be helpful, mentioned that he and Donna had recently gone to Selleck, Washington to see friends, and that perhaps she had gone there.

RULE, ANN

Ann Rule (1931-2015) has a unique place in the Bundy story as she was once a co-worker at a crisis clinic where they fielded calls from those calling in seeking help, and later friends. Once Ted Bundy became a suspect in the murders of women from Washington State and beyond, she was, like many who knew Ted Bundy, unconvinced of his guilt. However, as time passed, she would, like others, come to see that Bundy was in fact the killer so many investigators had been looking for. That also led her to write what became a best-selling book, *The Stranger Beside Me*.

SALT LAKE CITY, UTAH

Salt Lake City, Utah, would play a large role in the Ted Bundy murders. Not only would Bundy put down roots here and live a "normal" outward life as he had in Seattle, but also like Washington, he would terrorize the state for the entire time he was there.

SAMPSON, THOMAS

In 1973, Ted Bundy was hired by the Seattle Crime Prevention Commission by the director, Thomas Sampson. Bundy's tenure there would be rather brief (about five months), and he would move on. However, the two men again worked together in 1974 for the Department of Emergency Services, where they were co-workers. When Sampson was later interviewed by the Thurston County Sheriff's office, he spoke highly of Bundy, which isn't surprising, as Bundy had a good reputation with almost everyone he worked with over these years.

SANDPIPER TAVERN

The Sandpiper Tavern, located at 722 N.E. 45th Street in Seattle's University District, is where Ted Bundy would meet Liz Kloepfer in September 1969. This location has served as a tavern since 1941 and began as The Rainbow Tavern and continued as such into the 1960s, at which time it became the Sandpiper Tavern. In 1973, it switched back to the Rainbow and in the years that followed, it became a popular spot for big-name bands and singers.

SARGENT, ROBERT

On Sunday, July 14, 1974, Bob Sargent and his girlfriend, Nancy Battema, decided to go to Lake Sammamish State Park for the day. To that end, they called their friends, Kenneth Little and Denise Naslund to see if they'd like to join them for the day. Ken and Denise said yes, and after meeting at a local tavern for a beer, they'd leave Sargent's car at the bar and they'd go in Denise's car to the park. The group arrived at Lake Sammamish between 1:00 and 1:30 p.m. By 4:30 p.m., Denise would encounter Ted Bundy, and having fallen for one of his ruses, she was led away to her death.

SCHMIDT, MIRIAM JOAN

Miriam Joan Schmidt and Kathy Parks shared room 325 in Sackett Hall at Oregon State University. On the evening of May 6, 1974, both Miriam and Kathy had plans to visit with other students in room 334 around 11:00 p.m., but as they were leaving (she would later tell authorities), Kathy told Miriam to "go on" and then said she'd join them later. Miriam Schmidt then departed for room 334. Feeling a bit concerned, however, she returned to their room about 15 minutes later and Kathy was gone.

SCONYERS, WILLIAM DALE

William Dale Sconyers was a desk clerk at the Holiday Inn in Lake City, Florida, and would, along with fellow desk clerk, Randy Alton Jones, check Bundy into the hotel at 8:44 p.m. and he was registered into room 433. By this time in his life, Bundy was going downhill emotionally and mentally, and it showed. According to Sconyers, Bundy was, "greasy, dark, and dirty…[he] looked weird…."

SEATTLE, WASHINGTON

Seattle, Washington in many ways is Ted Bundy; at least for those who study this complex and voluminous case. Although at the end Bundy admitted to (but refused to name) murdering a hitchhiker in or near Tumwater, Washington (south of Seattle), in 1973, Bundy's "launch" into full time murder began in Seattle with the Karen Sparks bludgeoning and attempted murder on January 4, 1974.

Ted Bundy would end his time as a resident of Seattle on September 2, 1974, as he traveled to Salt Lake City, and where he would become a resident, law student, and murderer. He would never again live in Seattle or anywhere else as a resident of the state. He would return home a few times over the next year and a half, with his longest stay being his time home between November 1975 and late January 1976, at which time he would return to Utah to stand trial for the abduction of Carol DaRonch. Once this occurred, Bundy would never again set foot in Seattle or any other location in the state of Washington, or the Northwest.

SEATTLE CRIME COMMISSION

Ted Bundy worked for the Seattle Crime Commission between November 1972 and April 1973. During his time there (as well as the work he did for the Department of Emergency Services), Bundy was always secretly on the hunt for information concerning how the police operated with each other in different jurisdictions, as well as any other area where he might acquire info that he could use to stay ahead of the police once he was up and running as a destroyer of women. Bundy must have been very impressed with himself for having worked at a governmental agency that had the "crime" in it, for when he was taken from jail in Salt Lake City and transported by Detective Jerry Thompson and crew to his apartment where he would sit on a couch while they searched his place, Thompson said he "kept saying things like, 'I know you guys have it tough, and I'll help in any way I can.... I know this work is rough.... I was on the Seattle Crime Commission.'"

SEATTLE CRISIS CLINIC

In September 1971, Ted Bundy went to work for the Seattle Crisis Clinic. Although it is difficult to separate myths from facts as to how good he was at this job, or what his real intentions were for working there (being a psychopath and a soon-to-be killer of women), it appears he was somewhat successful as a counselor, at least on occasion. More importantly, it would be here where he would meet Ann

Rule, and the two would strike up a friendship that would last for years.

SEATTLE YACHT CLUB

Ted Bundy worked at the Seattle Yacht Club from September 1967 until January 1968. His job there was parking attendant, so it can be assumed that despite whatever meager salary he received, Bundy likely received tips as well. According to Sybil Ferris, an elderly woman who befriended Bundy, it was Ted's constant stealing of food that would bring his job to a screeching halt. What follows is from Dr. Al Carlisle's book, *A Violent Mind: The 1976 Psychological Assessment of Ted Bundy.*

He was six weeks at the Yacht Club and they let him go. He wasn't supposed to eat the food, but he was always in the pantry eating all the fresh foods and whipped cream he could get and all the fancy foods he could eat. He would grab them and take them to his locker. He was always in trouble with them.

Sybil Ferris was incorrect that he was there only six weeks, but her story of Bundy's theft of food fits perfectly with what we know about him - his penchant for stealing whenever the opportunity presented itself, be it food or anything else.

SEGUN, YOMI

After Ted Bundy attacked four women at the Chi Omega sorority house (killing two) in the early morning hours of January 15, 1978, he headed out the front door still gripping the bloodied log he'd used during the beating of his victims. As Bundy shut the front door of Chi Omega, it was approximately 3:15 a.m. Bundy, not satiated with the carnage he'd created at Chi O, started walking in the direction of Dunwoody Street, located only five blocks from the sorority house.

At 3:20 a.m., as Yomi Segun drove west along Jefferson Street, he spotted a man that he'd later identify as Ted Bundy who was, in his mind, acting suspicious. Detective D.L. West, said the following concerning Segun's testimony:

Mr. Segun states that he observed a white male about 5'10" and about 160 lbs. wearing light brown pants, a blue coat and a dark colored knit cap walking fast westerly on Jefferson Street.... This subject had brown hair and a pointed nose. He was carrying something in his left hand and holding it close to his left leg.

Bundy would make it to Dunwoody Street, where he climbed through a window and attacked Cheryl Thomas with the very same log Yomi Segun saw him carrying only minutes before. It is certain that Bundy knew where he was going, and authorities rightly believe that the attack on Cheryl Thomas was a premeditated attack. Even Cheryl Thomas, in a 2018 documentary, states she believed she'd seen Bundy before, and that perhaps, he'd ridden a bicycle past her house one day.

SEVERSON, BRYAN

Bryan Severson, the youth who "purchased" Bundy's VW but wouldn't be allowed to keep it very long.

In 2016, I interviewed Bryan Severson, who, at the age of 17, purchased Ted Bundy's beige, 1968, VW Beetle. Bundy had posted an ad in the *Salt Lake Tribune* and Bryan, having spotted it, went over to Bundy's apartment and agreed to buy the car. Unbeknownst to young Severson, Bundy's bail bond company held the original title, so Bundy found a way to make a passable copy and he hoped it would pass Severson's "inspection." and he'd be on his way with $800 in his pocket. In other words, he was scamming the kid in the same way he'd been scamming people for most of his life.

What follows are some interesting incidents from Bundy's "sale" of his VW to Severson and the full story of his interactions with Bundy can be found in, *The Bundy Secrets: Hidden Files on America's Worst Serial Killer*:

On September 19, 1975, Ted Bundy climbed into his VW for the last time and traveled south to Sandy, Utah, to finalize the deal with Severson, who couldn't wait to have his new car. When Ted arrived, he discovered that Severson needed to wait a couple of hours for his mother to return home so that he could cash the $800 check he'd received from his loan company. Extending a gesture of hospitality, he suggested they go inside his home and wait. Naturally, it wasn't ideal to wait on the front steps for two hours. However, Severson recalls that after only five or ten minutes, Bundy became noticeably uncomfortable, so they went back outside to the front steps. This was not the only odd reaction Severson would see about Bundy. When his police officer neighbor came out of his house, Severson went over to speak with him, and Bundy began showing signs of nervousness. Although noticeable, Severson stated that he didn't give it a lot of thought at the time. Later, of course, it would all make perfect sense.

Bundy also did something that had nothing to do with nervousness, but which did strike Severson as a bit strange. A female neighbor, who was also a friend of Severson, came walking down the sidewalk and Bundy locked his eyes on her and kept up that gaze the entire time she moved all the way down the block.

Once the deal was done, Bundy thanked him for buying his car. Because Bundy had shown up without anyone to drive him home, Severson gave him a lift back to his apartment. Bundy also told Severson that he should just drive the VW but not transfer the title as the tags wouldn't expire until January of 1976, a move that would allow Severson to delay licensing and tax payments. Given the understanding that Bundy never made suggestions to benefit other people when his own intentions were at stake, the real reason for his offer undoubtedly had more to do with making it more difficult for the cops to locate and bring the car in to search it for additional evidence.

SHARP, THERESA MARIE

Theresa Marie Sharp, 26, was at Lake Sammamish on July 14, 1974, and sat within 10 to 15 feet of Janice Ott that morning. She happened to notice that she wore short, blue jean Levi cutoffs, and an "off-white mid-riff blouse." Sharp also told authorities that after she removed the clothes covering her bikini, she put on cocoa butter, and that directly in front of her, the woman had laid her bright yellow 10-speed bicycle on the sand. What follows is taken directly from her statement to police:

A guy came walking up to her. He said something thing about a sailboat. It sounded like, Will you help me with my boat, or Would you like to ride in my boat. The girl sort of hesitated, but then said can I bring my bike with me. He said, sure, okay. She thought the boat was at the lake, and he said no, it was at his parents' house. She looked like she wasn't going. I couldn't hear what was said then, but then I heard her say, under one stipulation, that I meet your parents. He said, sure. Then she said I don't know how to sail. He said that's OK, it will be easy to teach you. She asked him if there was room in the car for the bike. He said it will fit in the trunk. She got up, slipped her blue-jeans and her top on, and then she picked up her beach bag..... The two of them then left.

SHEPARD, RAELYNNE

Raelynne Shepard was the drama teacher at Viewmont High School in Bountiful, Utah. On the evening of November 8, 1974, Raelynne would encounter Ted Bundy while passing through the crowded foyer of the school's theater as she was hurrying about with last-minute details prior to the start of the play, *The Redhead*. By the time Bundy saw Shepard, the play had already drawn some 1500 people, and many of them were in the process or had already taken their seats in the auditorium.

Exposing himself to so many people apparently didn't concern Bundy, but it also must be remembered that less than an hour before, Bundy had abducted Carol DaRonch, stopped and attacked her in front of the McMillan Elementary school, lost control of her which allowed her to escape and be picked up by an older couple. All that said, it should be noted that Bundy, already in that somewhat detached altered-state of murder, where he believed he had his victim secure only to lose her, propelled him to seek out a victim immediately. And because he had previously (two weeks earlier) obtained a brochure at the Bountiful Recreation Center advertising the Viewmont High School play, *The Redhead*, it popped into his head and he knew right where to go.

To whatever degree he was moving in that adrenalin-filled altered state of murder is unknown. But given that he appeared a bit agitated and somewhat forceful (as well as odd) in his interactions with Raelynne Shepard, it's most likely he was. And given the fact that he was always one for bold moves even prior to the entering of that altered state of murder, it seems that the combination of both made him appear strange during particular moments while he was either in the auditorium or in the foyer. And Bundy's talking to Raelynne Shepard on several occasions that night made it that much easier for her to identify him once she was contacted by the police.

SHERROD'S

Sherrod's was a very popular bar/discotheque located next door to the Chi Omega sorority house which is located at 661 West Jefferson Street in Tallahassee, Florida. Many Chi Omega residents frequented Sherrod's and in fact, Bundy had attempted to ply his trade of abduction and murder with the females at the club. But instead of drawing women to him as was the case when he was in the Pacific Northwest, it was said by those who saw him that his eyes looked weird, and he was generally creeping the women out and repulsing them. What follows is from *The Bundy Murders: A Comprehensive History*:

Oddly, both Margaret Bowman and Lisa Levy had been at Sherrod's that evening. Whether Bundy actually saw them is unknown, but he was well aware that members of the sorority frequented this club, as well as other nightclubs in the area. It is also of interest that sometime between midnight and when Sherrod's closed on the night of the murders, an "unknown male" called out to a young woman who was passing in front of Sherrod's and said, "Are you a Chi O?" When she told him no, that she belonged to another sorority, he responded rather cryptically, "You're lucky."

SILVERTHORNE, COLORADO

Ted Bundy was a creature of habit, and this was discovered after his arrest and his gas credit card purchases came before the eyes of investigators. In that record, detectives saw that Bundy would often stop in the same locations, even if nothing particular was happening in said location. As to Silverthorne, Colorado, records indicate that he stopped there on two of his trips to Colorado, the last being on the 5th of April 1975. The next day, Bundy would wander into Grand Junction, Colorado (Bundy would purchase gas in the city), where he would abduct and murder Denise Oliverson. The distance between Silverthorne and Grand Junction is a hair over 176 miles. When you look at all the locations where Bundy sought victims in the state, he was using I-70 in his attempt to traverse the state.

SIMPSON, LARRY

Larry Simpson was the lead prosecutor for the Chi Omega murders. And in April 1979, it would be Simpson who offered Ted Bundy the best deal he was ever going to get: life in prison with no possibility of parole. And to that end, Simpson approached Mike Minerva, Bundy's lead defense attorney, with the offer that if Bundy would stand up in open court, and confess to the murders of Margaret Bowman, Lisa Levy, and Kimberly Diane Leach, he would be spared the death penalty and the certainty of two complicated and drawn out trials. Bundy at first accepted the deal but then rejected it in open court, thereby ensuring his death in Florida's electric chair.

SKAVIEM, KAREN

Karen Skaviem was a roommate in the same rooming house as Lynda Ann Healy, and Karen's room was, like Lynda's, in the basement, and their rooms were separated by a plywood wall, which gave the basement two distinct bedrooms. On the night/early morning that Lynda disappeared, Karen went downstairs to her room and Lynda's room was dark and Karen believed she was sleeping. She would later tell the police that she believed she fell asleep around 1:30 a.m. and that she heard nothing unusual that night.

In the morning, she was awakened at 5:30 by Lynda's alarm but she remained in bed until her clock started buzzing at 6:00. At 6:30 a.m., the phone rang, and it was Northwest Ski Promotions, Lynda's employer, asking why Lynda wasn't at work. When Karen went to Lynda's room to check on her, she not only found that Lynda was gone, but she also noticed that Lynda's bed was made. That, in and of itself, was unusual, as it was not Lynda's habit to make her bed during the week, as she had little time to get ready and get to work on time. Understandably, when Karen Skaviem and the others learned that the disappearance of Lynda was foul play, they could not stay at the home any longer and sought out living quarters elsewhere.

SMITH, JOLENE

Jolene Smith (1959-2014) was the sister of Melissa Smith, abducted and murdered by Ted Bundy. She is also the one who informed investigators (Colorado detective Michael Fisher, in particular) that the makeup and nail polish her sister was wearing when her body was discovered did not belong to her sister. This gave rise to the theory that Bundy was applying makeup to the bodies, as well as washing their hair.

SMITH, CHIEF LOUIS

Midvale, Utah Chief of Police, Louis Smith (1927-1985), was the father of Melissa Smith, and the good friend of Detective Jerry Thompson of the Salt Lake County Sheriff's Office. When his daughter Melissa disappeared on Friday, October 18, 1974, Chief Smith understood that she had been abducted, as Melissa wouldn't have "taken off" or otherwise run away from home. When her body was discovered on a rough hillside in Summit County by a couple of hunters, the chief would turn the investigation over to Jerry Thompson, who was already working the other cases pf missing and murdered women in the state.

SMITH, MELISSA ANN

Melissa Smith (1957-1974), because of a quick change of plans, became a victim of Ted Bundy on October 18, 1974. It was a Friday night and Melissa had plans to attend a sleepover. Had this occurred, we would never have heard her name, and she might be alive today with children and grandchildren. But that had abruptly changed, and worse still, no one had called Melissa. When Melissa telephoned her friend that was hosting the sleepover, the phone at the friend's house just kept ringing, and it was obvious to Melissa that no one was home. However, another friend who was having boyfriend problems, called Melissa and asked her to come up to the Pepperoni Pizza Place restaurant where she was working, and so, in Melissa's mind, the night would not be a total waste.

What follows are three small sections from three of my books on the case. I will let these sections speak for themselves, and I will add clarity when needed. The last section will contain information that has remained unknown (outside of the detectives) and unpublished until the publication of my third Bundy book, *The Bundy Secrets: Hidden Files of America's Worst Serial Killer*, published in 2017. It pertains to my interview with Louise Cannon who knew Bundy (he was trying to date her), and she saw him at a bar only two hours before he abducted Melissa Smith. We begin with my book, *The Bundy Murders*, and we pick up where Melissa agrees to meet her friend:

Although naturally upset that her plans for Friday night had come to a screeching halt, the night would not be a complete waste. A friend of Melissa's had called wanting her to come to the nearby Pepperoni Pizza Place. Melissa would do what she could to help her emotionally distraught friend who had recently lost a boyfriend. Within minutes, she set off on foot into the night and would arrive unharmed at Pepperoni a short time later. Sometime around 9:00 P.M., Melissa called home to tell her sister Jolene she'd "be home around ten." This was the last contact Melissa would have with her family.

Her route home would be the same, although there is the possibility she intended to catch a ride part of the way, as at least one witness said he saw her hitchhiking about the time she should have been heading home (when her father learned of this he was quite upset, as he had warned her of the dangers). If this is true, Bundy may have been there to lean over and pop open the passenger door for the grateful and smiling young lady, and that would have been the easiest and the safest way for him to abduct her.

But if she walked home, she did have to cross by, or go over the grounds of a middle school, where there were gaps in the lighting, and it would be near here that a witness, standing out in her front yard at that unlikely hour raking leaves, would hear a scream pierce the night air around 10:15 P.M. If this was the terrified cry of Melissa Smith, then Bundy captured her much as he overpowered Nancy Wilcox, except there is little doubt that from the moment Bundy saw Melissa, he intended to murder her just as he murdered all the others. If he did abduct her during that walk home, it may well have started in the pizza restaurant, with Bundy eyeing her from another booth. Later, after Bundy had been identified in the press, a witness emerged who told police that a person he believed to be Bundy sat in the booth just behind Melissa and exited almost immediately after she left the restaurant. Although it's never been firmly established that Bundy was in the pizza eatery that night, it is very likely he was. Situated close to State Street, a main drag running north and south for miles and filled with hordes of young *people cruising in their cars or walking past the shops and restaurants, it's just the kind of place Bundy liked to be.*

It is this writer's opinion that Bundy followed her home using his VW, and at some point, drove past her, and at the appropriate spot, stopped his car, grabbed the crowbar and hid. And just as Melissa passed by, he lunged at her and quickly struck her with the crowbar. Melissa, seeing a man intending to harm her with that crowbar, had time to let out one scream only, and the woman raking leaves at that hour heard this scream.

What follows next is a portion of the report from the investigation of the murder of Melissa, and it's the report of Detective Ben Forbes. Melissa's body was discovered on October 27th, nine days after Bundy abducted her. However, Forbes estimates the time of her death only about 36 hours earlier. If this is the case, it's likely Bundy kept her in an unconscious state for some five to seven days, and given the time involved, most likely either inside his apartment (no smell as she's not yet dead), or in a cellar area that is covered with a locked covering to which Bundy had a key. She may have been in the cellar only, but the room is also something Bundy would have undertaken (see it as the Lynda Ann Healy in reverse); and this is given credence as while Bundy would normally leave his room unlocked at his 565 First Avenue apartment in Utah, there were times when surprised visitors found his door *uncharacteristically* locked. In any event, this location likely housed a number of his victims for a time, and these would be Melissa Smith, Laura Ann Aime, and Debra Kent, whom Bundy admitted at the end taking her "up to my apartment."

Now, here is Detective Forbes' report:

Victim: Smith, Melissa

Address: 180 Fern Drive, Midvale, Utah

ELEMENTS OF INVESTIGATION: Body of a young white female American found on a hillside in the oak brush east of Summit Park Subdivision in conditions which would lead investigating officers to believe that this is an obvious homicide. Mountainside covered in oak brush.

WEAPONS USED: One navy blue sock used for the purpose of strangulation; some type of blunt instrument, possibly a rock.

Discovered by PHILLIP D. HUGHES. Further details on Mr. Hughes are contained in Sheriff Ron Robinson's report. It [the victim's body] was found by Mr. Hughes in the location described in item #3

At approximately 4:00 p.m. on 10-27-74, this reporting officer received a phone call from Sheriff Ron Robinson of Summit County informing me that he had a homicide on his hands and that the nude body of a young white female American had been found on a hillside east of Summit Park Subdivision by some deer hunters. At this time he requested my assistance at the scene. He also informed me that he had attempted to contact Capt. Hayward through the office but had been unsuccessful. I informed Sheriff Robinson that I would respond to the scene and make attempts to contact Capt. Hayward. After I hung up the phone from talking to Sheriff Robinson, I called Capt. Hayward's residence and he had already been informed of the situation, and he himself was en route to the scene. We agreed to meet at the Skyline Café at the Summit Park Subdivision. When we arrived at the Skyline Café in Summit Park, we were met by Sheriff Robinson and some of his deputies and were led into the scene of the actual crime.

The crime scene will be as follows:

The location of the crime scene is approximately due east of the Summit Park Subdivision, bordering Timberline Subdivision. The actual area of the crime scene itself is mainly predominated by fairly heavy scrub oak and innersparsed (sic) small pine trees. In some fairly tall scrub oak is the body of a white female American, present age unknown, appears to be about 5'4" to 5'5" tall, approx. 110 to 115 pounds. Auburn-reddish hair. Around the neck of the victim is a necklace made of wooden beads, mostly yellow with blue and red beads about every three inches around the necklace. Also around the neck of the victim is what appears to be a man's navy blue knit sock, and this is tied behind the neck of the victim. The body is located on its stomach with the left arm completely folded underneath the body and the right arm extended and unfolded at a 90 degree angle and both legs bent at the knees. There are heavy predominant abrasions over the left and right shoulder blades, and these extended down to almost the small of the back. There are also heavy abrasions on both buttocks and large scrape marks on both buttocks, with more abrasions on the left leg from the knee extending down approximately 8 inches towards the foot. On closer examination of the head of the victim, approximately 6 inches above the top vertebra is what appears to be a bullet wound of contact, approximately one-half inch by one inch, and this is circumferenced by powder burn of approximately one-eighth inch in diameter. There are what appears to be livermortis (sic) marks on the central part of the back, and as far as rigor mortis is concerned, the lower limbs are fairly rigid at this inspection, but the arms and hands are fairly limber. I would estimate the time of death anywhere from 30 to 36 hours.

As previously mentioned, I will be ending the information on the murder of Melissa Smith, with the testimony of Louise Cannon whom I interviewed for my book, *The Bundy Secrets*, and she tells of her running into Bundy at a local and popular Salt Lake City bar.

When I first interviewed Louise Cannon, I asked her if I was the first writer to interview her (as I'd never before heard her name or seen her story), and she said yes, adding that she had only given interviews to the various detectives who came calling after Bundy's arrest. Her full story, which contains all the interactions she had with Bundy, including this surreal chance meeting, hit the printed page for the first time with my book, and I'm very thankful to another valid

Bundy contact in Salt Lake City who gave me her contact info.

SMITH, NEVA

Neva Smith, a resident of Lehi, Utah, became an unlikely part, albeit a small one, in the record of the Ted Bundy murders. On June 26, 1975, Susan Curtis, 15, left her home in Bountiful, Utah along with two other female friends, and the trio set out on their bicycles for Provo, Utah, some 50 miles south of Bountiful. It was to be a two-day ride, and they were looking forward to attending the Bountiful Orchard Youth Conference, being held at Brigham Young University. On the first night of their trip, according to the Brigham Young University Police case file, Susan Curtis and her friends stayed "in a yard at the residence of Neva Smith of Lehi, Utah." The next evening, Susan Curtis, who had just eaten supper and had returned to her room to brush her teeth, would disappear as she crossed the campus on her way back to the banquet hall where her friends were waiting for her. According to a newspaper report, she made this trip in the "fading light."

SNYDER, AGENT JERRY

Jerry Snyder, a DEA agent, was at Lake Sammamish with his family (including their Doberman) on July 14, 1974, and sat some distance behind Janice Ott and witnessed the interaction that Bundy had with her a little before noon on that hot and clear Sunday. Because Snyder had charge of the dog, he had to sit about 30 feet back from his wife and kids who were closer to the water. What follows is a portion of his statement to King County Police:

Approximately 10:45 or 11:00 a.m., it was several minutes after we had been on the beach, I noticed a white male walking, he was to my right. Walking down the beach toward me and the reason I noticed him, or looked at him anyway, I noticed that he was looking at all the girls as he walked down the beach. He would stop, almost come to a complete stop, after he had walked up to a girl laying on the beach and as if what it appeared to me that he was trying to pick up a girl or trying to find someone that met with his qualifications. The man continued to walk up to me and then eventually walked past and stopped at the place where the girl with the black double piece bathing suit was laying down and he stopped and said something to the effect of "Hello, Miss" or "Excuse me, Miss" or words to the effect like that. And I don't recall any further conversation other than that he sat down in a cross-legged position and spoke with the young lady for maybe five minutes.

Unbeknownst to Agent Snyder, as the young woman rose to her feet and prepared to go with the man, he had no idea he had just witnessed the abduction of Janice Ott. Later, after Ted Bundy's capture and revealing to the world, Jerry Snyder would positively identify Ted Bundy as the man he saw stop and speak with Janice Ott, and eventually leave the park with her.

SOMMERS, DETECTIVE RICK

Detective Rick Sommers was one of the responding investigators to the crime scene containing the body of Melissa Smith. Lead detective Ben Forbes would do the examination of the body (at the time, they were not aware who was lying before them), and would write the report. For the full story see Smith, Melissa, or Forbes, Detective Ben, in this book.

SOUVIRON, DR. RICHARD

Dr. Richard Souviron, a forensic odontologist, made dental impressions of Ted Bundy's mouth after Sheriff Ken

Katsaris obtained a warrant to take the impressions so that they can be compared to the bite marks left on the body of Lisa Levy, one of the homicide victims from Chi Omega sorority house in Tallahassee, Florida on January 15, 1978.

SPRINGER, OFFICER CHUCK

Officer Chuck Springer, with the Florida State University campus police, was working as an operating room tech at Tallahassee Memorial Hospital on the day (early morning) of the attack at the Chi Omega sorority house in Tallahassee, and was present in the ER as the dead and injured were transported to the hospital. However, he had previously applied to become an officer with the FSU campus police, and within days after the attack he was hired. What follows are a couple of sections from Chuck's story that appear in *The Bundy Secrets: Hidden Files on America's worst Serial Killer*:

In February of 1978, at the time of the Chi Omega attacks, Chip Springer was working as an operating room tech at Tallahassee Memorial Hospital, and was present in the OR when the victims of Ted Bundy were treated. Jaws were wired back together, cheekbones were worked on, and the brains of the injured were monitored for swelling and bleeding. Doctors from their respective specialties worked well together, collectively providing the best possible care for the victims.

Even though Springer was working as an OR Tech, he had applied to become a police officer with Florida State University campus police, but the process was slow and he had to be patient. The day after the murders of Margaret Bowman and Lisa Levy at Chi Omega, however, an emergency hiring order was issued and he was told to report the next day. Before he reported for duty, they asked if he owned a firearm, and he replied that he did. After conferring with them, he was allowed to use it as his service weapon.

STANFORD UNIVERSITY

In the summer of 1967 (June through August), Ted Bundy attended on a scholarship Stanford University's Chinese Institute, believing his future included working to improve Chinese and US relations. He also believed his work would have included traveling to and living in Asia for periods of time. While at the university, Bundy rented a room or small apartment in Palo Alto. But Bundy would begin to falter academically and soon he would abandon his dreams of working in Asia. Bundy would allude to his life during this time when he admitted to Donald M. Hall, an adult probation and parole officer with the State of Utah, that he felt "a bit too alien" in his new home.

STEVENS, JOANNE

Joanne Stevens was a student at Oregon State University in Corvallis, Oregon. She was also a friend of Kathy Parks, who was abducted by Ted Bundy from OSU (by way of a ruse, he led her away) on May 6, 1974. Because Joanne knew Kathy's habits well, she was interviewed by campus police and informed them of Kathy's habit of walking around the campus late at night.

STONE, VALERIE

Valerie Stone and Carla Jean Black, both Florida State University students, entered Sherrod's, a disco bar situated directly next to the Chi Omega sorority house in Tallahassee, Florida, around 12:00 a.m. on January 15, 1978, and noticed a weird looking man they would later identify as Ted Bundy. For more about their experience, see Black, Carla Jean in this book.

STORWICK, TERRY

Terry Storwick, Warren Dodge, and Ted Bundy, had all been friends since they were young boys, and very often if you saw one of them the other two couldn't be far behind. Being in such close proximity of each other, and visiting each other's homes, it was inevitable that things would be seen that would create a life-long memory, and one of these would be an incident that Storwick witnessed and would later tell a writer. Being aware of the enmity that Ted often exhibited towards Johnny Bundy, and how Ted had the ability to spar verbally with his adoptive father and often get the best of him, Storwick watched Johnny take a swing at Ted one day, but he missed. Apparently, Bundy had the ability to set Johnny off given just the right amount of taunting.

Another oddity involving Terry Storwick has to do with Bundy's hunting for victims on more than one day at Central Washington State College in April 1974. Storwick had been living in Ellensburg since 1972 and attending college at Central, and was still attending additional classes at Central in 1974, and Bundy apparently knew his friend was still there. Given this fact, one would think that the possibility that he might run into Storwick while he was in the process of abducting and murdering a female, would concern him, but apparently not.

STOTLAND, DR. EZRA

University of Washington professor, Dr. Ezra Stotland, met Ted Bundy in 1968 when he stopped supporting the Democratic candidate for president and became part of an independent group supporting the nomination of Nelson Rockefeller for president. Apparently, Dr. Stotland liked Bundy and had him out to his house on numerous occasions. And the family liked Bundy as well, except for the doctor's 15-year-old daughter who once quipped that she "didn't like his act." Stotland's younger daughter, however, liked Bundy, and Bundy would sometimes entertain her by pitching the child up in the air.

STOTT, ROBERT

Robert Stott was a member of the prosecution, headed up by Deputy District Attorney, Dave Yocom, during the trail of Ted Bundy for the abduction of Carol DaRonch from the Fashion Place Mall, on November 8, 1974.

SUMMIT COUNTY, UTAH

Summit County, Utah plays a part in the Bundy case as it was in this county that the body of Melissa Smith was discovered on October 27, 1974. For the full story of this murder, see Smith, Melissa in this book.

SUTHERLAND, MONICA

Monica Sutherland was a housemate of Lynda Ann Healy, in a rooming house they shared with three other friends. On the morning it was discovered that Lynda had disappeared, Northwest Ski Promotions, Lynda's employer, called to ask where she was. Karen Skaviem called upstairs to see if anyone knew where Lynda was, and Monica called back down that she might be with her boyfriend, but the others said no, Lynda wouldn't do that.

SWINDLER, CAPT. HERB

Herb Swindler had been a cop for three decades when, on June 11, 1974, he became head of the Seattle PD homicide unit (he had come from missing persons). That particular day would be very busy for him, as in the early morning hours of that June 11th, Georgann Hawkins disappeared as she was walking down the alley behind Greek Row to go to her sorority house. It was a baffling case as Georgann had just spent 30 minutes talking with her boyfriend at the frat house on the corner, and as she was leaving, the second-floor window opened, and she spoke with Duane Covey for a few minutes. Once their conversation ended, Duane moved away from his window, and Georgann had only a short distance to walk before she could enter her sorority house.

At the time of the Georgann Hawkins disappearance, Seattle PD had had been working the Lynda Ann Healy disappearance as well. But Swindler, who was aware of the disappearances of other women around the state – women who were not from his jurisdiction and would not be part of his investigation – rightly believed there was likely a connection linking them all together, and that connection was an abductor and killer of women. Indeed, as the cases within the state started to mount: Lynda Ann Healy, Donna Manson, Susan Rancourt, Brenda Ball, and now Georgann Hawkins, the law enforcement community believed the chances of finding any of them alive were slim to none. They would never admit such a thing to the press or anyone in the public with such an ominous belief, but it was there nevertheless. And then came Lake Sammamish.

On a beautiful and sunny Sunday July 14, 1974, this abductor and killer of women made a bold move by abducting Janice Ott from the park around noon, only to return and abduct Denise Naslund around 4:30 p.m. It was an astounding move, and once again he'd gotten away with it. And the events of Lake Sammamish would seal the deal in the investigators minds that all of the missing girls were now dead. And while prior to this double abduction the authorities would never come out and speak of their fears so plainly, there would now be admissions here and there that the public would unavoidably find disconcerting. One of these showed up in the *Tacoma News Tribune* article of July 28, 1974, and it was a quote from Captain Swindler himself:

I lie awake at night thinking about those girls... I have a daughter too... I can sit here and spin theories all day," Swindler is quoted as saying, *"but none of them work without facts to go on... I wouldn't like to tell you some of the horrible suspicions I have – some of the strange theories I've wondered about... I'm at the point now where I'll do anything, no matter how improbable; we're as frustrated now as when we began."*

Since we are talking about the reaction from the police perspective concerning the missing women, and how Herb Swindler and others were trying to be delicate in their statements to the public, once the first body was discovered on September 7, 1974, all of that changed. What follows is a brief quote from my book, *The Bundy Murders*:

Although the sickening discovery of September 7 brought authorities no closer to finding the homicidal madman responsible for these killings, it did force the police to finally admit what they already knew to be true. Calling a press conference for a public whose fear was clearly escalating, Captain Nick Mackie of the King County Police Department, in a moment of rare transparency, admitted: "The worst we feared is true."

SYPHER, RICHARD

Richard Sypher was a reporter for the *Tacoma News Tribune* from the early 1970s through 1986. During those years he wrote articles pertaining to the missing girls, and once Bundy was on their radar, articles were written about Bundy and how the case against him was proceeding. Sypher also wrote a book about the downing of Korean Air flight 007, titled *Death Flight 007* published in 2002. Sypher served in the United States Army from 1966 to 1969.

TACOMA, WASHINGTON

Tacoma, Washington was the center of the universe for Ted Bundy for many years, and all of his formative years. Although Louise Cowell would take little Teddy when he was 4-years-old from her parents' house in Philadelphia, Pennsylvania to Browns Point, Washington, their ultimate destination would be 11 miles away in Tacoma. Soon after coming to Washington, Louise would meet Johnny Bundy and they would after a time, marry. And Johnny Bundy would adopt Ted and give him what is now his infamous last name.

In Tacoma, the main Bundy home for these formative years would be at 658 N. Skyline Drive, situated very close to the Narrows Bridge which stretches across Puget Sound. Here Bundy would explore his surroundings, and he and two friends, Warren Dodge and Terry Storwick, would become inseparable. Bundy would attend (when they were living at 1620 South Sheridan) Stanley Elementary, and when at 658 N. Skyline Drive, Geiger Elementary. Bundy then attended Hunt Junior High in Tacoma, and Wilson High School. By around the time he graduated from high school, in 1965, the Bundy's moved to a home at 3214 N. 20th Street in Tacoma. Bundy would also briefly attend the University of Puget Sound. After this, Bundy would move on to the life that awaited him in Seattle and the University of Washington.

Ted Bundy's boyhood home at 658 N. Skyline Drive, Tacoma, Washington

The Bundy residence at 3214 North 20th Street, Tacoma, Washington. The Bundy's moved here in the mid-1960s.

TALLASSEE, FLORIDA

Tallassee Florida was an unsuspecting city when Ted Bundy arrived there in early January 1978.

Upon arrival, Bundy used what money he had left and rented a room at 409 West College Avenue. It was a large two-story structure and looked like a typical old-style Southern home. Across its front was the name, The Oak, and Bundy settled in to his second-floor apartment. It was situated close to Florida State University, and the Chi Omega sorority house which Bundy would attack in the early morning hours of January 15, 1978, killing two women and seriously injuring two.

Not satiated with what he had done at Chi Omega, he walked five blocks and attacked Cheryl Thomas in her Dunwoody Street duplex apartment, but was unable to murder her because Thomas' next door neighbors were calling out to her through the thin walls and calling her phone, after they'd heard strange sounds like she was crying coming from her apartment. Bundy's total victim count in in Tallahassee would be three dead and two injured.

TANAY, DR. EMANUEL

Dr. Emanuel Tanay (1928-2014) was a forensic psychiatrist, and clinical professor of psychiatry at Wayne State University in Ann Arbor, Michigan, who performed an evaluation of Ted Bundy at the request of Michael Minerva, Bundy's lead defense attorney. From that interview came an insightful report about the mental and emotional make-up of the killer. What follows are portions of that report:

The extensive interactions which Mr. Bundy had with the police officers have not been carefully reviewed, however, even a cursory perusal of that material reveals that Mr. Bundy is driven by a variety of unrealistic motives such as playing games with the investigators for no other purpose than the sheer enjoyment of it. He challenges them and even taunts them. ...

The interview, the conference with defense counsel and the material reviewed reveal that Mr. Bundy functions in the role of "a chief counsel" and the public defender has been consistently manipulated into the role of "associate counsel." In his decision making process, Mr. Bundy is guided by his emotional needs, sometimes to the detriment of his legal interests. The pathological need of Mr. Bundy to defy authority, to manipulate his associates and adversaries, supplies him with "thrills," to the detriment of his ability to cooperate with his counsel....

In a certain sense, Mr. Bundy is a producer of a play which attempts to show that various authority figures can be manipulated, set against each other and placed in positions of internal conflict. Mr. Bundy does not have the capacity to recognize that the price for this "thriller" might be his own life. Mr. Bundy "the super lawyer" does not recognize that his client, Bundy the defendant, is not being adequately defended.

TAYLOR MOUNTAIN

Taylor Mountain is one of two known body dump sites used by Ted Bundy (there must be others, yet undiscovered, as Bundy admitted to burying certain victims, and these individuals have never been found) to discard the remains of his victims. Although it is a certainty that Bundy used Taylor Mountain as his first dump site (because of who was found there), it would not be discovered until March 1, 1975. Bundy's Issaquah dump site, discovered on September 7, 1974, was his second location.

One macabre aspect of the Taylor Mountain find was that it was the place where Bundy had deposited the heads of the four victims only. To set the tone of what the investigators were faced with, here is section from *The Bundy Murders*:

The killer had taken his victims as intact human beings, but this is not how they would be found. Only the lower mandible of Lynda Ann Healy was discovered at Taylor Mountain. Because her skull was not located, police could not determine if she had suffered the crushing blow that had now become a trademark of the monster.

In what was a surprise discovery for some, the cracked skull and lower mandible of Kathy Parks of Corvallis, Oregon, was also a part of the Taylor Mountain find. Being some 250 miles away from where she was last seen on that warm summer night of May 6, 1974, only added to the gruesome nature of the crime. That the killer reached out so far to claim a victim was yet another example of his unpredictability. Investigators noted that all of her upper teeth were missing.

During the search, Keppel would literally stumble upon the grinning skull of Susan Rancourt. Rancourt had suffered blunt force trauma to the back of her skull, and her mandible was broken in three places. Her long blond hair was found detached nearby.

The cranium, minus the lower mandible, of Brenda Ball was located. A portion of the right side of her skull was missing. It was the opinion of the medical examiner "that this was not caused by an animal."

As body dumps go, Taylor Mountain was not a substantial find, and it was immediately apparent to Keppel's people that this was merely the location chosen by the killer to discard the heads of his victims. Out there somewhere, they correctly reasoned, were the rest of the remains of these four women. It was a stark discovery, and one that wouldn't sit well with the public.

What was odd about this discovery, is that it was clear to Bob Keppel and his people that the killer had used the mountain to discard the heads only, which meant the bodies had been discarded —and probably buried--somewhere else. Bundy would later tell detectives that those victims he buried were never found, and it appears he knew the value of burial over simply discarding remains, as it keeps them out of sight forever. Because of this, a third Bundy dump site must be out there somewhere.

TELEVISION DOCUMENTARIES

Numerous Ted Bundy documentaries have been produced over the years, and what follows are some of the more recent additions:

Ted Bundy: The Death Row Tapes (2012) MSNBC
Ted Bundy: Devil in Disguise (2017) REELZ
Ted Bundy: Serial Monster (2018) REELZ
Notorious: Ted Bundy (2018) OXYGEN
Ted Bundy: How It Really Happened (2018) HLN
Ted Bundy (2019) ABC 20/20
Conversations With A Killer: The Ted Bundy Tapes (2019) NETFLIX
Ted Bundy: Mind of a Monster (2019) INVESTIGATION DISCOVERY

TEMPLE UNIVERSITY

After Ted Bundy was rejected by his girlfriend, Diane Edwards (identified in my book, *The Bundy Murders*, as Carla Browning), he left Washington State because he was inwardly imploding, and he returned to Philadelphia where his family members, the Cowells, lived. In fact, he lived with family at 4039 South Warner Street in Philadelphia. Bundy would enroll at Temple University in January 1969, but would only be there one semester, as he returned to Washington State in the spring.

TESTA, JOANNE

Joanne Testa was a roommate of Lynda Ann Healy in the rooming house they shared with three other women at

5517 12th Street N.E. in Seattle. On January 31, 1974, on the last evening of her life, Lynda Ann Healy made dinner for everyone in the house, and then afterward Joanne Testa, Lynda Healy, Ginger Heath, and their mutual friend, Pete Neil, walked the several blocks to *Dante's Tavern* at 5300 Roosevelt Way, where they'd take a table on the first floor. According to the statements from the others, Lynda would buy the first pitcher of beer. All four would have a good time relaxing and talking, and after a second pitcher was consumed, they'd head back to the rooming house as Pete needed to catch the 9:41 bus back to his place. And it is almost certain that Bundy took notice of them at *Dante's* and followed them home that early evening. He would also tell a writer later (speaking in the third-person), that he tried the front door of the rooming house and found it unlocked. Of course, he left after that, knowing he could come back in the middle of the night and move among the sleeping residents at that time.

When interviewed later by investigators as to their walk home, she said, "I do not recall anyone following us or approaching us on our way home."

By the next afternoon, with still no sign of Lynda, the police were called and the initial report was given to the patrolmen. But around midnight, a detective arrived and he went directly to Lynda's basement apartment. Joanne Testa followed close behind, and was there when he entered the room and went over to Lynda's perfectly made bed. What follows is taken directly from her statement to police: *I was there when the policeman pulled back the spread for the first time. I saw that the pillowcase was gone and that there were blood stains on the pillow and one fairly large blood stain on the sheet near the pillow... As far as I know, Lynda always kept a pillowcase on her pillow.*

Joanne Testa, like the other residents, would soon leave 5517 12th Street N.E. for what they believed (or at least hoped) would be safer quarters.

THOMAS, CHERYL

Cheryl Thomas, 21, was a student at Florida State University, and lived in a duplex at 431-A Dunwoody Street. Next door at 431-B, were two of her friends, and this would help her immensely on that pivotal night when Bundy attacked her.

It has been believed by authorities (and in my opinion, is true), that Bundy had been going on forays and looking into apartment windows even before the attack at Chi Omega on January 15, 1978. And police believe one of these windows was at 431-A Dunwoody Street. And then, in 2018, during an interview on a documentary, Cheryl Thomas mentioned that Bundy looked familiar, that she thought she's seen him somewhere. She then added that Bundy may have ridden a bicycle in front of her house and she saw him.

Nevertheless, in the early morning hours of January 15, 1978, after attacking the Chi Omega sorority – killing two and severely injuring two – he walked the four or five blocks to Dunwoody Street to attack Cheryl Thomas, and he did so by crawling through an unlocked rear window. His plan, of course, was to murder her while having sex with her from behind while he strangled her. However, she likely awakened, as Debbie Ciccarelli woke up to hear what sounded like her friend Cheryl pleading with someone and crying, followed by what she believed to be pounding noises. That pounding was Bundy beating Cheryl about the head with the same log he'd used to beat the women of Chi Omega.

Startled by what they heard, the neighbors started calling out to Cheryl through the thin wall separating the duplexes, as well as calling her phone. As such, Bundy was not able to carry out his plan of raping Cheryl while he strangled her to death. Foiled in his plans, he masturbated while Cheryl lay face down and unconscious on the bed (Bundy's semen stain would be found on the bed). As quickly as possible, Bundy went back out the window and began his walk back to his rooming house on College Avenue.

Thanks to the persistence of her neighbors, the police were already on their way. When found, Cheryl was in a semi-conscious state, and like Kathy Kleiner and Karen Chandler, Cheryl's jaw was shattered. She also suffered permanent hearing loss in one ear, and suffered from balance problems. This put an end to her desire of becoming a professional dancer.

Bundy was able to maintain fairly good grades and did well on tests. By fall of 1975, Bundy would be going through the monitions of going to school, but by now the police were starting to put the pieces together as to what he was, and soon his law student studies would be forever over.

UNIVERSITY OF WASHINGTON

The University of Washington would be central to Ted Bundy's life for a very long time. Having finished his freshman year at the University of Puget Sound, one would think his time at the U of W would have been an unbroken and sequential trek, but this was not the case. Bundy would enroll at the school only to withdraw on a couple of occasions, and he would not graduate from the university until June 1972, and he did so with a degree in psychology.

Red Square at the University of Washington
Courtesy Gina Wilmoth

VAHSHOLTZ, GEORGE

George Vahsholtz was an assistant to Colorado Deputy District Attorney, Milton K. Blakey, when they were attempting to bring Ted Bundy to justice. And in the course of this, the Colorado investigators and attorneys were working with their counterparts in Utah. As such, Vahsholtz was mainly responsible for working with Utah Deputy District Attorney, Dave Yocom.

VALDEZ, ANDREW

Andrew Valdez was a student at the Utah law school at the same time as Ted Bundy. However, because Bundy was only in class three times that first semester, when Valdez saw him that early January, he at first believed he was a transfer student. And after they introduced themselves to one another, a friendship began; or perhaps, more appropriately, Valdez liked Ted Bundy.

In the fall of 2018, I had the pleasure of interviewing Andrew Valdez for my book, *Ted Bundy's Murderous Mysteries*. What follows are some of the insightful things Andrew shared with me for the book, and they are a window into what it was like dealing with Ted Bundy both before he was arrested and after his incarceration.

During our phone conversation on November 12, 2018, Valdez told me he had at least two classes with Ted Bundy, one being contracts and the other, evidence. The first time he noticed Bundy was in January 1975, in his contracts class that was held in the afternoon, and he was sitting in the back row. When they spoke to each other, Valdez asked him if he was a transfer student, and Bundy said no. Bundy also mentioned he was from Seattle.

Valdez told me that Bundy looked like a "rich kid," and that he acted the part, as it were. He also mentioned that Bundy was a good dresser, but that often he would see Bundy wearing wrinkled clothes. Indeed, on that first day that they met, Valdez noticed that his turtleneck was wrinkled. When asked if his clothes ever appeared dirty, he said no, only wrinkled.

Although Bundy did begin coming to more classes that second semester, he still missed quite a few of them. Valdez said that Bundy came up to him one day and asked, "Do you mind if I look at your notes?" but he did one better and made copies for Bundy. Valdez said he made copies four or five times that winter for Bundy.

And after Bundy's first arrest...

The moment of Bundy's arrival at the Salt Lake County Jail around 3:00 a.m. on August 16, 1975, is a surreal one for both of the men involved, which neither man understood at the time. For Ted Bundy, it was the beginning of his unveiling, when he was being pulled out of the dark cover of the shadows, where his life would be changing forever.

But on this particular early morning, it was about two law students, who had already established a friendship, meeting at a time and place neither expected, and it would prove to be a line of demarcation for both men. When I asked Andrew Valdez about this odd moment, he said that after the initial greeting between the two men, he asked Bundy what had happened. Bundy initially told his law school buddy "I got lost," and would attempt to explain it a bit further over the next several minutes. Valdez noticed Bundy didn't appear nervous or concerned at all, and Bundy ultimately told Valdez what he'd already told arresting officer, Bob Hayward. Bundy said he'd been to see a movie at a drive-in and afterward he was just driving around; a story that didn't seem right to Valdez, who found it odd that Bundy had been driving around that area that late at night. Valdez also noted that his suspicion was not present solely because Bundy had been arrested, as he'd dealt with other law school friends who'd gotten arrested for one reason or another. His suspicion was based wholly on Bundy's less than credible explanation. Before the men separated, Bundy once again *asked Valdez to "take good notes," while at the same time saying he'd soon see him back in class.*

VALENZUELA, CAROL

Carol Valenzuela was reportedly last seen hitchhiking in Camas, Washington on August 2, 1974. It has been believed that Carol was a victim of Ted Bundy, but never proven nor confessed to by Ted Bundy. Her body was located on October 12, 1974 in a rural area of Clark County, Washington in the southern portion of the state. Found buried nearby was another female who was not identified until 2015.

That female, Martha Morrison, was finally matched by DNA provided by her sister and half-brother. But as to who killed her and Valenzuela (they were buried in separate graves but close to each other) was still up in the air, although Bundy was suspected of killing Valenzuela for many years. However, Warren Lee Forest, a killer who has been in prison for murder since 1979, once owned an air pistol which authorities have had in an evidence room since Forest's arrest. Because they now had a match that identified Morrison, they began digging through the evidence and they noticed blood on the handle of the air pistol. After sending the weapon to the lab it was conclusively determined that the blood on the handle was that of Martha Morrison. As such, it appears that Forest must be the killer of Carol Valenzuela as well.

VALINT, SYLVIA

Sylvia Valent, 15, along with a couple of friends, was at Lake Sammamish State Park on July 14, 1974. In fact, she sat only a few feet away from Janice Ott. And from what she told Det. Bob Keppel in an interview conducted at her home the following day, it was clear she paid attention to what was going on; which is something not always seen out of a

15-year-old kid. What follows is her report taken from the official report.

Taken by ROBERT D. KEPPEL
Statement of SYLVIA MARIA VALINT

On July 14, 1974, at about 1230 hrs., I was at Lake Sammamish State Park, with Kathy Veres and Pam. We were sitting on the beach close to the water. A girl I have positively identified as Jan Ott came up near me and she was on a bicycle. She laid her towel down; she had a pair of cut-offs and a shirt that was tied in the front that showed her stomach. The cut-offs were jeans. She had a dark colored knapsack. She took off her cut-offs and shirt and lay down. She had on a black bikini. I think she had leathered colored thongs. She lay there for about ½ hour.

Then a guy came up to her. He is about 5'6" to 5'7", medium-build, blondish-brown hair down to his neck, parted on the side, had dark tan, left arm in sling. The cast started at wrist and bent around the elbow. He had on white tennis shoes, white socks, white shorts, and a white "T" shirt. He said, "Excuse me, but could you help me put my sailboat onto my car because I can't do it by myself because I broke my arm." She said, "Well, sit down and let's talk about it. Where's the boat?" He said, "It's up at my parent's house in Issaquah." She said, "Oh, really, I live up in Issaquah." She said, "Well, okay." She stood up and put on her clothes. She picked up her bike and said, "Under one condition, that I get a ride in the sailboat." He said, "My car is in the parking lot." She said words like, "Well, I get to meet your folks then." He had asked her who she knew in Issaquah. They left like they were going out to the parking lot. They were only on the beach for about ten minutes. He had a small English accent, kinda like a fag. He had tiny sideburns. He was smooth talking. He was definitely a white male and could not be mistaken for a Latin or Hawaiian. His clothes looked like he was rich and dressed to go sailing. He stated that his name was Ted, after she said my name's Jan. I was *about two feet from Jan. We were about a hundred yards from the Rainier function. He walked up from the west.*

VAN DAM, PAUL

Paul Van Dam was the Salt Lake County prosecutor during Bundy's time in Utah. And it would be at a party hosted by Van Dam in June 1975, that he would meet Leslie Knutson (see Knutson, Leslie in this book). Van Dam's office would also be responsible for prosecuting Ted Bundy after he was charged with the abduction of Carol DaRonch; a trial that ended in a conviction for Bundy and a one to fifteen-year sentence in the Utah State Prison. Paul Van Dam would go on to become Attorney General of Utah, and would serve in this capacity from 1989-1993.

VIEWMONT HIGH SCHOOL

Viewmont High School, located in a nice neighborhood in Bountiful, Utah, was the site of the abduction of Debra Kent on the evening of November 8, 1974. Bundy, who had mishandled the abduction of Carol DaRonch when he led her away from the Fashion Place Mall, attacked her, and she got away, drove immediately to Viewmont High, where he knew a play, *The Red Head*, was showing where he hoped to obtain a victim (Bundy had learned of the play a couple weeks earlier after having picked up a brochure about it from the Bountiful Recreation Center.) And Bundy knew that where a high school play is, so are young women and girls. For the full story, see Kent, Debra, this book.

VON DREHLE, DAVID

David Von Drehle, a career and award-winning journalist, and currently Washington Post columnist, enters the Bundy story through his book, *Among the Lowest of the Dead: The Culture of Death Row*, and Ted Bundy is a part of the story.

VORTMAN, MARLIN

Marlin Vortman and his wife Sheila, met Ted Bundy during the political campaigns of 1972, and they quickly became friends. And because Bundy had his mask of sanity in place, neither Vortman or his wife noticed anything odd or deviant about him. As far as they were concerned, Ted Bundy was just a normal and friendly guy, they became good friends. But when the killer started to feel the heat of the police closing in on him, it would be Vortman the lawyer he'd call for advice. And Vortman, who at first believed the charges against Bundy were bogus, advised him of what his legal options were.

VOSHALL, LARRY

Larry Voshall (1944-1983) was, like Bundy, a politico in the Republican Party. However, his experience with Bundy did not leave him with the same enamored feelings often found in others who interacted with him. And once Bundy began coming to light as the possible killer of the Northwest, Voshall expressed his feelings to a mutual friend, and Bundy's possible role in the murders. What follows is a portion of Larry Voshall's statement to police:

While we were rafting to the Diversion Dam, his personality seemed to change. It was like he wasn't concerned about our safety or our enjoyment of the trip. He had tied an inner tube... to the back of the raft with some rope he got from his car. Becky rode in the inner tube and at one point he untied the rope, holding the inner tube to the raft and this initially frightened Becky very much.... During the trip I observed Ted Bundy wasn't very friendly and this did not seem like the Ted Bundy I had heard about.

Larry Voshall would hold various positions with the Washington State Republican Party, including assistant director at the Department of Emergency Services; staff director for the Republicans of the State House of

Representatives; and communication director for Republican members of the Washington State Senate. Voshall, who previously had heart issues, died of heart failure at the age of 39, on June 26, 1983.

WALSH, WILBER AND MARY

Wilber and Mary Walsh enter the Bundy story as they were the elderly couple that on November 8, 1974, were driving down the road known today as Fashion Boulevard (which runs behind the Fashion Place Mall in Murray, Utah), when all of a sudden, they saw a women appear in their headlights running towards then, and as they came to a stop where she was, Carol jumped into their car. Hysterical, Carol DaRonch kept saying a man tried to kill her. Wilber and Mary Walsh immediately drove her to the Murray Police Department. Attached to her right wrist were two handcuffs. They did not see the Volkswagen speeding away. Bundy, who had lost control of the abduction, headed north for Bountiful where he hoped to find a victim at Viewmont High School.

WARNER, DETECTIVE BOB

Detective Bob Warner, of the Salt Lake County Sheriff's office, was part of the team of officers and detectives involved in the search of Ted Bundy's apartment at 565 First Avenue. This search was of particular interest, as certain pieces of circumstantial evidence was obtained from Bundy's second floor apartment at this time. What follows is taken directly from Detective Jerry Thompson's report:

Criminal Homicide – Melissa Smith

On 8-21-75 this officer made contact with Theodore Robert Bundy, DOB 11-24-46, who lives at 565 First Avenue # 2, phone 531-7286. He was in the county jail at this time, taken out by Sgt. Bernardo and Detective Bob Warner. They met me at the county jail at approximately 6:30 p.m. Previous to this time, a consent search of his home was signed by him and Detective Forbes. We went to the individual's home, which is an upstairs apartment, and searched the home. As we entered the door, there was a pair of skis and a ten-speed bicycle, white in color, brand Peugeot, serial number 1695468. The apartment was very immaculate, in this detective's opinion. The individual had a small room made into an office with a desk and had numerous amounts of law books, several cases on the laws of evidence and criminal proceedings. A thorough search was made of this apartment by myself and Sgt. Bernardo. The only thing of significant value to this detective, which was taken by this officer, was a book called, "The Joy of Sex," a road map of the state of Colorado, a Colorado Ski Country Guide 1974 and 1975, a brochure from the Bountiful Recreation Center, a copy of a Chevron gasoline bill listed to THEODORE ROBERT BUNDY, and also a copy of a phone bill for the month of June, which listed a telephone call to Denver, Colorado....

In an unbelievably foolish move, Bundy had kept the Ski Country Guide despite the fact that he had made a mark at the Wildwood Inn! This, of course, is where he had abducted Caryn Campbell and murdered her some 2.8 miles from the Wildwood Inn. Now, that ski guide was in the hands of those who were trying to figure out what Ted Bundy really was. And when Jerry Thompson informed Colorado Detective Mike Fisher about the mark at the Wildwood Inn, Fisher barked over the phone, "You're shitten' me, Jerry… that's the place where our girl went out!" That "girl" was Caryn Campbell.

WATERS, STEVE

When the nude body of Caryn Campbell was discovered on February 17, 1975, the authorities converged upon the scene. Lead Detective Mike Fisher was there, as was District Attorney, Steve Waters. As they looked down at the frozen and partially eaten body, Waters, who knew Fisher very well, said, "Fish, you'll never find out who did this. You've got nothing to work with." It would be a daunting task, and Fisher knew it. But he was in this investigation until the end, he was confident at some point, her killer would be brought to justice.

WEBSTER, KERRY

Kerry Webster, whose name headlines some of the articles written about the Bundy case, started working for the *Tacoma News Tribune* in 1973 and remained with the paper for eight years. He would also work for the *Seattle Times*, *Seattle Post Intelligencer*, *NPR*, and the *Los Angeles Herald-Examiner*, to name a few. As of July 2019, Webster is the editor of *The Peninsula Gateway* in Gig Harbor, Washington.

WEEKS, KIM

Kim Weeks was a Chi Omega sorority sister in Tallahassee, Florida. She was also the roommate of Margaret Bowman who was murdered by Ted Bundy in the early morning hours of January 15, 1978. Fortunately for Kim, she was away for the weekend and this no doubt saved her life. Had she been asleep in her bed, Bundy would not have missed that opportunity and would have attacked her.

WEINER, DIANNA

Dianna Weiner was Ted Bundy's civil attorney and was responsible for handling his affairs, both towards the end of his life, as well after he was put to death. She also shows up in the record as being involved with the scheduling of Bundy's end-of-life confessions to the various investigators who had come to Florida at his request, and was watchful to see they ended on the agreed upon time.

WEST, OFFICER D.L.

Officer D.L. West, of the Tallahassee Police Department, was one of a number of officers investigating the Chi Omega murders, all under the watchful eyes of lead investigator, Donald Patchen. On the night of August 28, 1978, he interviewed a Yomi Segun, who stated that as he was driving down West Jefferson St (Chi Omega's street) at approximately 3:20 a.m., he noticed a man walking quickly down the sidewalk, and it appeared to Segun that the man was trying to hide something behind his leg (this would be the log/murder weapon he'd carried from Chi Omega). This caused him to briefly slow his car to see if he could get a better look at the individual. Segun would describe him almost the exact same way Nita Neary described the man who came down the steps at the sorority house. Later, after Bundy's arrest, Mr. Segun was shown photographs and was able to identify Bundy as the man he saw that early morning.

WEST, HELEN

Helen West appears in the official record of the Ted Bundy murders simply because Bundy had become lax with his political duties in 1974. Detective Roger Dunn's official report states that not only had Ted Bundy missed the King County convention that was being held in the Seattle Center, but he missed the Republican state convention on July 5-6 as well. His report states, "the 1st alternate delegate, Helen West had to represent the 43rd pct. for him."

WILCOX, NANCY

Nancy Wilcox, 16, (1958-1974) was the first to die in Utah by the hands of Ted Bundy. At least, this is what authorities believe. Towards the end of his life, Bundy admitted to murdering eight people in Utah but he only admitted to five victims by name. Therefore, we can assume Wilcox was the first victim, but without the additional names, we cannot know this for a certainty. In any event, there are two scenarios out there on how Bundy abducted her. The first is that she got into his VW as someone supposedly saw Nancy in a yellow VW. The other, and in this writer's opinion is the correct one, is that Bundy was driving down a darkened street and spotted her walking along the sidewalk, and what follows matches fairly well with what he told a writer in the third person many years later.

It was October 2, 1974, and Nancy Wilcox was walking down a darkened suburban neighborhood in Holliday, Utah, when just by chance, Bundy spotted her as he drove his VW slowly down the street. Bundy, who had quickly stopped his car, would later say he grabbed a knife and it was intention to rape the young girl only. When he grabbed Wilcox, he said he forced her off the sidewalk and into a darkened orchard. Here he tried to disrobe her but she struggled with him. When she wouldn't stop arguing with him, and when putting his hand over her mouth didn't work, Bundy said he started choking her. Once she was out (dead, of course), he removed her clothes and sexually assaulted her. Bundy would later say he didn't know if she was dead when he left her. It was only after he returned several hours later and saw her lying there, did he know for sure that she was dead. Bundy never spoke about it, but he had to have loaded her body into his car and taken it to a location where she could be buried or left in a very rural location where he could leave her nude and let the animals devour her remains until there were only bones scattered over a wide area.

WILDWOOD INN

The Wildwood Inn in Snowmass, Colorado, plays a big part in the Bundy murders because of the abduction and murder of Caryn Campbell, a nurse from Michigan, on January 12, 1975. It was an unusual abduction (as many of

Bundy's abductions were), and a number of human factors caused the event to unfold the way that it did.

Ted Bundy would tell Colorado detective Mike Fisher that he drove around Aspen that day for several hours, and then went up to the lodges in Snowmass Village to walk, as the article said, "amongst the lodges" on crutches and holding ski boots in an attempt to attract a female to help him. He then ended up at the Wildwood Inn near the pool and was trying to get the attention of a particular woman who just might succumb to his wiles as an injured skier, and help him to his car (which was parked in the large parking lot on the side of the inn) so he could whack her in the head and take her away. The woman, however, wasn't interested.

At the same time, Caryn Campbell, having taken the elevator up to the second floor, was walking across the second-floor walkway, when, through the wafting steam coming off the outdoor heated pool, spotted the "injured" man holding ski boots and walking on crutches and offered help. Bundy said yes, and when they reached the parking lot, Bundy hit her in the head with the ski boots and knocked her out. Within minutes Bundy had taken her to a spot along Owl Creek Road some 2.8 miles away, and rape and murder her. He would leave her body in the snow just a short distance from the road.

WINKLER, OFFICER HENRY

Officer Henry Winkler of the Tallahassee Police Department was on the scene after the attack on the Chi Omega sorority house in the early morning hours of January 15, 1978. His duties while in the sorority were to dust for prints in the rooms where the attack occurred, as well as photographing the scene. When he entered room 8 that was shared by Kathy Kleiner and Karen Chandler, he was met with a horrific scene. What follows is from Sgt. Winkler's report: *This writer proceeded to room #8 and observed blood on both beds. Blood was also located on walls around both beds and on the ceiling between the windows and light fixture.*

WINN, STEVEN

Steven Winn is an American journalist and co-author of the book, *Ted Bundy: The Killer Next Door.*

WOODROW WILSON HIGH SCHOOL

Courtesy Gina Wilmoth

Woodrow Wilson High School at 1202 N. Orchard Street in Tacoma, Washington, was the high school Bundy attended and graduated from in 1965.

There is an interesting, and what appears to be an impromptu, photograph taken of Bundy on the day he graduated from Woodrow Wilson High School, where he stopped on this walkway. The black and white photo is grainy but still a good shot. And this is that walkway and Bundy was standing about a foot in front of the walkway separating line closest to the photographer, with his feet almost touching the grass. (Courtesy of Gina Wilmoth)

WOODS, ROBIN

Robin Woods was a good friend of Denise Naslund, and on July 30, 1974, she sat for an interview with the police and her testimony is part of the official record.

WORTHINGTON, JACK

Jack Worthington was a sailor who had survived the Second World War, and most likely, was the father of Ted Bundy; or, Teddy Cowell, as he was known at his birth. I say most likely, as it's never been determined who his father was, but the police generally believed Worthington to be his father.

YAKIMA RIVER

The Yakima River will be remembered to readers of the Bundy case as the body of water that was used by Ted Bundy and his girlfriend, Liz Kloepfer, to go rafting. Indeed, Bundy had rafted on the river with other friends as well, and it has always been a popular rafting river by the locals. But it would be the raft trip he took with Liz that would stand out as a very strange event; an event that sparked, for unknown reasons, his murderous nature coming to the surface, and which may have been a sign that Bundy's ability to control the darkness within was slipping.

July 6, 1974 was a beautiful day with lots of sun and a blue sky. Their trip down the Yakima was looking like it was going to be a good one. They'd brought a lunch with them and would stop along the way and have a lunch on land. Up until the time they pulled up to shore to have lunch, things had gone well. But Liz started to notice that Bundy was growing quiet now, and he appeared to be daydreaming. Unbeknownst to Liz, his mind was returning to murder- either the murder that lay before him at some point, or perhaps a mental excursion into the past, about the murders he'd committed, and as such, his growing quiet and withdrawing from her was the natural reaction of the predator revisiting the private activity he enjoyed the most. However, as this genie of murder was rising, it would not be satisfied with memories only. Soon, a strange manifestation would try to engulf Liz.

Once Liz and Bundy were back in the raft, the moodiness and virtual silence continued. And before an hour was out, Bundy, without warning, pushed Liz into the cold water of the Yakima. Liz would later say that when she came to the surface, Bundy's face was blank, and it was as if he wasn't seeing her. Fortunately, the genie would recede and Bundy would become himself again. But in little more than a week, he'd be hunting at Lake Sammamish, and Janice Ott and Denise Naslund had but eight more days to live.

YOCOM, DAVID

Deputy County Attorney, David Yocom, was responsible for the prosecution of Ted Bundy for the kidnapping of Carol DaRonch. Bundy was represented by John O'Connell. The trial, which began in February 1976, would last five days. It was not a normal trial, where the result was in the hands of a 12-person jury. Bundy and O'Connell, because of the notoriety of the case, believed it would be very difficult for the accused to have a fair jury trial anywhere in Utah. So, they decided to go with what is known as a bench trial, meaning, Judge Stewart M. Hansen, considered to be a scrupulously fair man, would hear the evidence and make a decision based on the evidence alone, and Judge Hansen did so. Bundy was convicted for the abduction of Carol DaRonch and sentenced to one to fifteen-years in the Utah State Prison.

YOUNG, NANCY

Nancy Young was the roommate of Debbie Ciccarelli in their half of a duplex (431-B) they shared with Cheryl Thomas (431-A) on Dunwoody Street in Tallahassee, Florida. For the full story of the attack on Cheryl Thomas, see Thomas, Cheryl.

ZIMMER, BRUCE

Bruce Zimmer was the dean of the law school at the University of Utah. Bundy, who enrolled for the 1974-1975 school year, was absent nearly the entire first semester, attending class on only three occasions. Dean Zimmer would later say of Bundy that he was "viewed as a student with a slightly below grade point average."

AFTERWORD

Having finished this encyclopedia of the Ted Bundy murders, in what has become a series of five books covering all aspects of this case, it is the perfect time to bring this many-year journey into this most infamous case to an end. In looking back, I can truly say I never saw any of this coming. I never expected to write even a paragraph about Bundy. But in May 2005 I met retired detective Jerry Thompson of the Salt Lake County Sheriff's Office, and my life changed forever. From that meeting, the desire hit me to write a biography of Ted Bundy, and that produced my break-out book, *The Bundy Murders: A Comprehensive History*, in 2009.

And then, in 2015, because some folks that were connected to the case had either passed away, or were otherwise ill, I decided to write a companion volume to my first book, which became *The Trail of Ted Bundy: Digging Up the Untold Stories*, published in 2016. 2017 brought to light the second companion volume to first book, *The Bundy Secrets: Hidden Files on America's Worst Serial Killer*, and in early 2019, in what I believed would be my last excursion into the life of Theodore Robert Bundy, *Ted Bundy's Murderous Mysteries: The Many Victims of America's Most Infamous Serial Killer,* was published. After four books I just "knew" that would be it for me and that I was forever finished with Ted Bundy! But alas, it was not to be. I had just one more book to write, and this encyclopedia is that book.

Thank you, again, to all of you who have followed along with me through the years. And a hello to all of the recent readers of my books on the case as well. It will be an interesting journey for you as every one of my books carry new testimony and new information that was uncovered along the way.

It has been a fantastic journey, and I'm happy I listened to my heart each time I had a decision to make on whether I should write a new Bundy book. And listening correctly in each case gave me a wind to my back which carried me through to the completion of all five books. That wind has now settled down, signaling, I believe, that my work on Ted Bundy is now complete. However, should that wind begin to stir once again within me, being driven by new discoveries, questions, or controversies (so common to the Bundy case) my future may yet deliver another book on this most infamous serial killer. And I have learned well to never say never again.

Lastly, I want to thank Shirl Sipperley DiGugno, who once again assisted me by locating certain information that made my work load just that much lighter, and when you're writing a book, that's always nice. Thanks goes also to Gina Marzano Wilmoth, who took some photographs of pertinent locations in Washington State that appear in this book, and to Francine Bardole, who provided much-needed photos from several locations in Salt Lake City, Utah. And of course, I want to mention one more time, Michael Rinehart, who contacted me and explained his idea that I should write an encyclopedia of the Ted Bundy murders. It was great advice, Michael, and I'm happy I followed it!

Thanks again, everyone!

See more Ted Bundy pictures online in the gallery: **http://wbp.bz/teottbmgallery**

For More News About Kevin Sullivan, Signup For Our Newsletter:

http://wbp.bz/newsletter

Word-of-mouth is critical to an author's long-term success. If you appreciated this book please leave a review on the Amazon sales page:

http://wbp.bz/teottbma

ENTRY INDEX

A

Africano, Julius Victor	9
Aime, James "Jim" Junior	9
Aime, Laura Ann	9
Aime, Shirly Tolton	10
Alameda Junior High School	10
Anderson, C.L.	11
Anderson, Chief Dean O.	11
Anderson, Larry	11
Aspen, Colorado	13
Augerson, Officer Terrance	14
Austin, Dr. Van O.	15
Aynesworth, Hugh Grant	15

B

Bailess, Professor Tim	16
Baird, Nancy	16
Baldridge, Detective William	16
Ball, Brenda Carol	17
Bardole, Francine	18
Barnard, Kent	18
Bartholomew, Carol	19
Bartholomew, Wynn	19
Battema, Nancy	20
Beal, Detective Ira	20
Beer, John	20

Black, Carla Jean	21
Blackburn, Donald Edwin	21
Blackburn, Ferol Lorraine	21
Blakey, Milton K.	22
Bodiford, Detective Steve	22
Boise, Idaho	23
Books	23
Boone, Carol	24
Bountiful, Utah	25
Bowman, Margaret	25
Brannon, Officer Oscar	26
Brigham Young University	26
Burnham, Steve	27
Browne, John Henry	27
Bundy, Glenn	27
Bundy, Linda	28
Bundy, Louise	28
Bundy, Richard	29
Bundy, Sandra	29
Bundy, Johnny Culpepper	29
Burr, Ann Marie	30
Burr, Beverly	31
Burr, Donald	32

C

Campbell, Caryn Eileen	32
Cannon, Louise	34
Carlisle, Dr. Al	36
Carter, Mike	36
Cascade Mountains	36
Central Washington State College	37
Chapman, Detective Norman	38
Chez Pierre	38
Chi Omega	38
Ciccarelli, Debbie	39

Clark, Dr. Donald M.	39
Cleckley, Hervey M.	40
Colquitt, Sharon	40
Corsaletti, Lou	40
Covey, Duane	41
Cowart, Judge Edward	41
Cowell, Jack	43
Cowell, John	43
Cowell, Samuel	43
Culver, Lynette	44
Cunningham, Julie	46
Curtis, Jane	47
Curtis, Susan	48

D

Dante's Tavern	49
DaRonch, Carol	50
Davis, Ross	52
Dawes, Deputy Keith	52
Dawson, Dr. Paul	53
Dekle, Bob	53
Denver, Colorado	53
Dickey, Officer Roy	54
Dobson, Dr. James	55
Dodge, Warren	55
D'Olivo, Kathleen	56
Doros, James	59
Dowdy, Nancy	59
Dunn, Detective Roger	59

E

Elizabeth Lund Home for Unwed Mothers	60
Ellensburg, Washington	61
Ellis, Megan	61

Elway, Stuart	61
Erickson, Chuck	61
Evans, Governor Dan	62
Evergreen State College	63
Everitt, Randy	63

F

Fargo, Lorraine	64
Farmer, Millard	66
Ferris, Sybil	66
Fife, Officer John	67
Films	67
Fisher, Detective Michael	67
Fletcher, Art	68
Fonis, Detective Ted	68
Forbes, Detective Ben	69

G

Gadowski, Dr. Raymond	70
Gage, Russell	71
Garfield County Jail	71
Garzaniti, Rickey	73
Gay, Jerry	73
Gellatly, Marvin	74
Glenwood Springs, Colorado	75
Graham, Janice	76
Grand Junction, Colorado	76
Griggs Lumber Mill	77

H

Hagen, Chris	77
Hagmaier, William	77
Hall, Donald M.	78
Hammons, Elzie	78

Hanson, Judge Stewart M.	79
Harbor View Mental Health Center	79
Harter, Elizabeth	79
Hawkins, Georgann	81
Hayward, Sgt. Bob	84
Hayward, Captain Pete	84
Healy, Lynda Ann	85
Heath, Ginger	86
Heffron, Laura	87
Henderson, Paul	88
Holley, Sheriff Mack	89
Homer, John	89
Holmes, Ronald M.	90
Horn, Andrea Michelle	90
Hughes, Phillip	91

I

Idaho hitchhiker murder	91
Idaho State University	94
Intermountain Crime Conference	95
Issaquah, Washington	95

J

Jacksonville, Florida	96
Jones, Randy Alton	96
Jopling, Judge Wallace	96

K

Kaehler, Sharon	97
Katsaris, Sheriff Kenneth	97
Kent, Belva	97
Kent, Dean	97
Kent, Debra	98
Kent, William	101

Keppel, Detective Robert D.	101
Kessler, Ken	101
Killien, Phil	102
Kleiner, Kathy	102
Kloepfer, Elizabeth	103
Knutson, Leslie	105
Kralicek, Deputy Rick	107
Kraut, Dawn	108

L

Lake City, Florida	110
Lake Sammamish State Park	110
Laramie, Wyoming	113
Larsen, Richard W.	113
Leach, Kimberly Dianne	113
Lee, Officer David	114
Legal Messengers, Inc.	115
Leidner, Charles	116
Levy, Lisa	117
Lewis, Dr. Dorothy Otnow	117
Lindvall, Detective Matt	118
Little, Kenneth	118
Lohr, Judge George	119
Lubeck, Bruce C.	119

M

Mackie, Captain Nick	119
Manson, Donna Gail	120
Matthews, Gary	122
McBride, Dr. Stanley	124
McChesney, Kathy	124
McClure, Ralph	124
McKibben, David Allison	124
McMillan Elementary School	125

McPhee, Christy	125
Mentzer, Dr. Richard H.	126
Merrill, David	126
Messier, Francis	127
Meyers, Undersheriff Ben	127
Miami, Florida	127
Michaud, Stephen G.	128
Miller, Officer Mitch	128
Miller, Ralph	129
Minerva, Michael	129
Misner, Kenneth Raymond	130
Moon, Officer Keith L.	130
Moore, Jacqueline	131
Morris, Frank	132
Mott, Sgt. Edward O.	133
Mottram, Robert H.	133
Murray, Utah	133

N

Nampa, Idaho	133
Naslund, Denise	134
Neil, Pete	136
Neary, Nita	136
Nelson, Melanie	137
Nelson, Polly	138
Newkirk, Officer Henry	139
Norman, Dr. Art	139

O

O'Connell, John	140
Oliverson, Denise	140
Olympia, Washington	141
Ondrak, Detective Daryle M.	142
Oregon State University	142

O'Reily, Kevin 142
Ott, James 143
Ott, Janice 144

P

Palumbo, Henry 145
Parks, Kathy 146
Parmenter, Danny 147
Parmenter, Leslie 148
Patchen, Detective Donald 149
Payne, Officer Gerald 150
Ped Line Medical Supplies 151
Pensacola, Florida 152
Philadelphia, Pennsylvania 152
Pitkin County Courthouse 153
Plischke, Jacqueline 154
Pocatello, Idaho 155
Porter, Officer Donald 157
Price, Utah 158
Provo, Utah 158

R

Rafferty, Cheryl 159
Rancourt, Susan Elaine 160
Rankin, Elza E. 162
Reichert, Dave 162
Reneau, Russ 163
Roberts, Jennifer 164
Robertson, Shelley 165
Robinson, Sheriff Ron 165
Rock Springs, Wyoming 166
Rogers, Ernst and Frieda 167
Rose, Greg 168
Rosellini, Albert 169

Ross, Tony 169
Rule, Ann 170

S

Salt Lake City, Utah 170
Sampson, Thomas 171
Sandpiper Tavern 171
Sargent, Robert 171
Schmidt, Miriam Joan 172
Sconyers, William Dale 172
Seattle, Washington 172
Seattle Crime Commission 173
Seattle Crisis Clinic 173
Seattle Yacht Club 174
Segun, Yomi 174
Severson, Bryan 175
Sharp, Theresa Marie 177
Shepard, Raelynne 178
Sherrod's 179
Silverthorne, Colorado 179
Simpson, Larry 180
Skaviem, Karen 180
Smith, Jolene 181
Smith, Chief Louis 181
Smith, Melissa Ann 182
Smith, Neva 187
Snyder, Agent Jerry 187
Sommers, Detective Rick 188
Souviron, Dr. Richard 188
Springer, Officer Chuck 189
Stanford University 190
Stevens, Joanne 190
Stone, Valerie 190
Storwick, Terry 191
Stotland, Dr. Ezra 191

Stott, Robert 192
Summit County, Utah 192
Sutherland, Monica 192
Swindler, Capt. Herb 192
Sypher, Richard 194

T

Tacoma, Washington 195
Tallassee, Florida 197
Tanay, Dr. Emanuel 197
Taylor Mountain 198
Television Documentaries 200
Temple University 200
Testa, Joanne 200
Thomas, Cheryl 202

U

University of Washington 203

V

Vahsholtz, George 204
Valdez, Andrew 204
Valenzuela, Carol 206
Valint, Sylvia 206
Van Dam, Paul 208
Viewmont High School 208
Von Drehle, David 208
Vortman, Marlin 209
Voshall, Larry 209

W

Walsh, Wilber and Mary 210
Warner, Detective Bob 210

Waters, Steve	211
Webster, Kerry	212
Weeks, Kim	212
Weiner, Dianna	212
West, Officer D.L.	213
West, Helen	213
Wilcox, Nancy	213
Wildwood Inn	214
Winkler, Officer Henry	215
Winn, Steven	216
Woodrow Wilson High School	216
Woods, Robin	217
Worthington, Jack	218

Y

Yakima River	218
Yocom, David	219
Young, Nancy	219

Z

Zimmer, Bruce	220

Other Ted Bundy Books From Kevin Sullivan and WildBlue Press

The Trail of Ted Bundy: A look into the life of serial killer Ted Bundy, from those who knew him, to those who chased him, and from those who mourned his many victims. The Trail of Ted Bundy: Digging Up the Untold Stories, is a journey back in time, to a world when Ted Bundy was killing young women and girls in the Pacific Northwest and beyond. You'll hear all the revealing stories; many of them coming to light for the first time. *wbp.bz/trailbundya*

The Bundy Secrets: The hidden files of the manhunt to find and stop Ted Bundy, as well as the investigations into his depredations, gathered from official and unofficial sources from Washington to Florida, as well as contemporary interviews and author commentary to flesh out the details. A must-read for true crime students of Ted Bundy. *wbp.bz/bundysecetsa*

Ted Bundy's Murderous Mysteries: Written by the foremost authority on Ted Bundy, this latest examination of this brutal serial killer contains new, revealing, and never-before published interviews with those close to Bundy, close to his victims, and a potential victim who barely escaped his clutches. *wbp.bz/tbmma*

More Great Reads From Kevin Sullivan and WildBlue Press

VAMPIRE: The Richard Chase Murders is the tale of a diabolical, homicidal madman running amok, mutilating and murdering the unsuspecting residents in the quiet neighborhoods of Sacramento, CA. His diabolical and unrelenting desires, not just to kill his victims but to drink their blood, unleashed a terror within the city unlike anything the residents had ever known. *wbp.bz/vampirea*

Kentucky Bloodbath: An excursion into the weird and the bizarre: from a medieval-esque murder in a small town museum to the jilted boyfriend who decided that his former girlfriend needed to die on her twenty-first birthday. Then there's the demented son who returns home to live with his mother and stepfather, and one night in their beautiful mansion sitting atop a high bluff overlooking the Ohio River, slaughters them. Each case will keep you on the edge of your seat. *wbp.bz/kba*

AVAILABLE FROM CHRISTIAN BARTH AND WILDBLUE PRESS!

THE GARDEN STATE PARKWAY MURDERS by CHRISTIAN BARTH

http://wbp.bz/tgspma

See even more at:
http://wbp.bz/tc

More True Crime You'll Love From WildBlue Press

RAW DEAL by Gil Valle

RAW DEAL: The Untold Story of the NYPD's "Cannibal Cop" is the memoir of Gil Valle, written with co-author Brian Whitney. It is part of the controversial saga of a man who was imprisoned for "thought crimes," and a look into an online world of dark sexuality and violence that most people don't know exists, except maybe in their nightmares.

wbp.bz/rawdeal

BETRAYAL IN BLUE by Burl Barer & Frank C. Girardot Jr.

Adapted from Ken Eurell's shocking personal memoir, plus hundreds of hours of exclusive interviews with the major players, including former international drug lord, Adam Diaz, and Dori Eurell, revealing the truth behind what you won't see in the hit documentary THE SEVEN FIVE.

wbp.bz/bib

THE POLITICS OF MURDER by Margo Nash

"A chilling story about corruption, political power and a stacked judicial system in Massachusetts."–John Ferak, bestselling author of FAILURE OF JUSTICE.

wbp.bz/pom

FAILURE OF JUSTICE by John Ferak

If the dubious efforts of law enforcement that led to the case behind MAKING A MURDERER made you cringe, your skin will crawl at the injustice portrayed in FAILURE OF JUSTICE: A Brutal Murder, An Obsessed Cop, Six Wrongful Convictions. Award-winning journalist and bestselling author John Ferak pursued the story of the Beatrice 6 who were wrongfully accused of the brutal, ritualistic rape and murder of an elderly widow in Beatrice, Nebraska, and then railroaded by law enforcement into prison for a crime they did not commit.

wbp.bz/foj